"Wow!" Your Belief Quotient delivers all of the components of shifting beliefs which includes research to results. Dr. Lisa Van Allen shares with conviction the step-by-step actions to shift your beliefs from scarcity and fear to abundance and faith. This book can and will change your life!"

—CHERYL E. BURGET, Founder/CEO of Your Intended Life

"Your Belief Quotient is a great asset to those who have been searching for powerful tools to make positive changes in their lives. I love the balance of concepts delivered and descriptive stories to support the concepts. There is nothing like a good story to remember a concept. Everyone reading this book will have a power tool in their hands to make lasting changes for themselves and others."

—BETH K. LEREVRE, CEO of Master Life, Inc.

"In the Passion Test we teach that "What you put your attention on grows stronger in your life." Dr. Lisa has shown us how to put our attention on the beliefs that build us up and eliminate focus from those beliefs that get in our way. When we strengthen and build better beliefs we are free to fulfill our destiny and manifest the life of our dreams."

—JANET BRAY ATTWOOD, New York Times
Bestselling Author of The Passion Test - the
Effortless Path to Living Your Life Purpose

"Beliefs are our foundational understanding about the world. They impact how we approach everything, including whether we see ourselves as heroes or victims in our own life story. Deftly weaving threads from psychotherapy, counseling, and coaching, Lisa offers a sound paradigm and clear pathway for identifying your negative beliefs and stopping them in their tracks. In this book, we can learn practical tools and skills for shedding these negative beliefs and creating the lives we truly desire. If you want to learn how to stop sabotaging your success, get this book. Read it. And apply it."

—RACHNA D. JAIN, PsyD, Author,
Overcome Rejection: The SMART Way

"Dr. Lisa Van Allen's book will convince you that strengthening your beliefs is necessary to have a successful and fulfilling life. Being more of a rational than emotional decision maker, I learned both the value of following my passions and how to identify them. There are many writers and speakers today who communicate these principles, but Dr. Lisa tells us why and how to make the changes we know we need to make. Having coached many executives and business owners, she has real world experience that lends real-world credibility to her book."

—BILL JOHNSON, Division Manager of Sales Process Improvement, Hewlett Packard

"The Belief Quotient is a refreshing read for anyone desiring more out of life. Dr. Lisa's easy-to-follow guide provides the reader with the necessary tools to grow useful and empowering beliefs, while arming the with the courage and techniques to crush limiting beliefs. Thanks to the principles outlined in this book, my life, my relationships, and my business have become more fulfilling than I could have ever imagined. This book is a MUST READ!"

—DAVE SHEFFIELD, speaker, author, coach.

"All I can say is: WOW. This book will completely shift how you think about your life and career. For me, the content and impact of Dr. Lisa's book ranks right up there with Stephen Covey's *7 Habits of Highly Effective People.* Your Belief Quotient is joining my list of "must read" book for all my clients."

—JULIE PERRINE, Founder and Chief Excellence Officer of All Things Admin

Your Belief Quotient

7 Beliefs that Sabotage or Support Your Success

Lisa Van Allen, PhD

Copyright © 2013 Lisa Van Allen, PhD.

All rights reserved. No part of this book may be used or reproduced by any means, graphic, electronic, or mechanical, including photocopying, recording, taping or by any information storage retrieval system without the written permission of the publisher except in the case of brief quotations embodied in critical articles and reviews.

The Belief Quotient and the Belief Quotient Assessment is a trademark owned by Dr. Lisa Van Allen. All other trademarks are property of their respective owners.

Winner of the 2011 Transformational Authors Contest

Balboa Press books may be ordered through booksellers or by contacting:
Balboa Press
A Division of Hay House
1663 Liberty Drive
Bloomington, IN 47403
www.balboapress.com
1-(877) 407-4847

Because of the dynamic nature of the Internet, any web addresses or links contained in this book may have changed since publication and may no longer be valid. The views expressed in this work are solely those of the author and do not necessarily reflect the views of the publisher, and the publisher hereby disclaims any responsibility for them.

The author of this book does not dispense medical advice or prescribe the use of any technique as a form of treatment for physical, emotional, or medical problems without the advice of a physician, either directly or indirectly. The intent of the author is only to offer information of a general nature to help you in your quest for emotional and spiritual well-being. In the event you use any of the information in this book for yourself, which is your constitutional right, the author and the publisher assume no responsibility for your actions.

Any people depicted in stock imagery provided by Thinkstock are models, and such images are being used for illustrative purposes only.
Certain stock imagery © Thinkstock.

Printed in the United States of America

ISBN: 978-1-4525-6635-1 (sc)
ISBN: 978-1-4525-6637-5 (hc)
ISBN: 978-1-4525-6636-8 (e)

Library of Congress Control Number: 2013900119

Balboa Press rev. date: 2/08/2013

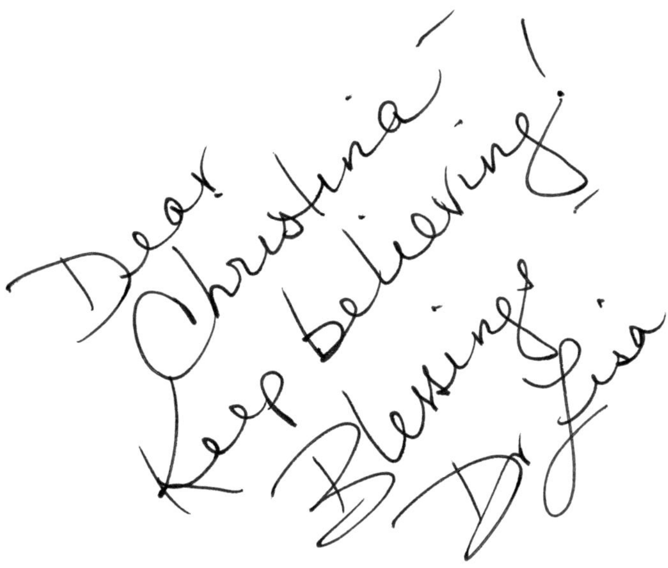

. . . we are only as free as our beliefs allow us to be.
~Sasha Xarrian

Completing this project was a major milestone in my life and could only be accomplished because of the people who helped me build better beliefs:

Thank you to my parents, Terry and Rhoda McElree, who in the midst of turmoil and of joy always managed to make me feel valued and capable of succeeding at anything I wanted to do. I am resilient because of you.

Thank you to my own Duke Dierks. The connection we have grows deeper and more meaningful every day. I couldn't have done this without you!

Thank you to the inspirational coaches and teachers who have mentored and challenged me through the years to take inspired action and initiative. You made me believe I could and should write this book. Christine Kloser, Dr. Daniel Amen, Rhonda Britten, Val Bullerman, Lynette Patterson, Melanie Hoffner, Beth Lefevre, Janet Bray Attwood, Chris Attwood—you have each touched and encouraged me in my beliefs.

Thank you to Julie Perrine, Suzanne L. Bird-Harris, Amy Belice, Louis and Melissa Collins and Serena Collins. This project shines because of your excellence in art, editing and design.

Thank you to my clients for allowing me to walk with you on this journey of belief and your willingness to share your stories. Thank you for sharing from the abundance of your hearts.

Thank you to my teachers and friends at Harvest Life, Willowcreek, and Orchard Hill Churches. Thank you for helping me to overcome my fears and strengthen my faith.

Most of all, thank you to my God and Savior who created me with a purpose, filled me with passion, and provided every resource I need to believe, achieve and succeed.

CONNECTING

Join us in creating better beliefs at **www.BeliefQuotient.com**

I love social media! Let's keep in touch:
www.Facebook.com/TheBizDoctor
www.Twitter.com/LisaVanAllen
Twitter hashtag for *Your Belief Quotient* is #beliefquotient
www.LinkedIn.com/in/LisaVanAllen

Continue the journey beyond the book and access these resources at www.BeliefQuotient.com

- Boundless Riches Workbook
- Audio and video interviews of luminaries who have strengthened and built better beliefs
- Resource Lists

TABLE OF CONTENTS

Introduction xiii

Chapter 1 The Beginnings of Belief 1

Chapter 2 Your Belief Quotient 21

Chapter 3 Rebuilding Resilience 51

Chapter 4 Creating Connectedness 77

Chapter 5 Increasing Initiative 109

Chapter 6 Expanding Excellence 129

Chapter 7 Accepting Abundance 145

Chapter 8 Finding Faith 177

Chapter 9 Pursuing Purpose 197

Chapter 10 Strengthening New Beliefs 223

Resources 229

Index 237

INTRODUCTION

"Belief is a magical word because it is the beginning of all successes." Napoleon Hill

Beliefs are the lens through which everything you experience is filtered. Like a set of eyeglasses, the right prescription can help you see your way to success while damaged or faulty lenses impair your ability to function. *Your Belief Quotient* will help you to understand how your beliefs were formed and how they can be transformed.

Are your beliefs supporting or sabotaging your success?

- Do you often feel like your own worst enemy?
- Do you sometimes find your own behavior puzzling?
- Do you succeed once and then never seem to be able to capture that level of performance again?
- Do you find yourself troubled by anger, worry or fear?
- Do you feel like you are stuck and unable to move forward?
- Do you feel like you are hiding behind a mask, afraid of being found out?
- Do you have dreams/vision/goals, but fail to achieve them?

If you answered "Yes" to any of the questions above, your life is being held back by negative beliefs.

Whether it's a small glimmer of hope or a bright light shining in your soul, you know you can be so much more than you are. You want to be more of yourself—more of who you were designed to be. You set intentions, establish goals, make plans, adopt strategies, and work very, very hard. You have gifts, talents and strengths that help you achieve some measure of success. But then it shows up again—that knack you have for sabotaging your success. Sometimes you are surprised by your own behavior. "Where did that come from?" you wonder, as you watch yourself acting as if an alien has invaded your body and taken control. Words come out of your mouth that you never planned to say. Emotions erupt making you feel out of control, embarrassed, and ashamed. It is enough to drive you to over-eat, over-sleep, over-spend, or over-indulge in any number of self-defeating, addictive behaviors to cover your shame and silence the voice inside that says "you can't do it, you are a failure."

You have not been possessed by an alien. What you are experiencing is your own unconscious mind breaking through and doing everything it can to survive. Your unconscious self sees change as a threat to its existence. Every time you attempt to stretch yourself or move in a new direction, your unconscious self checks in to see how this new world fits with your old beliefs. If the unconscious sees no threat or challenge to your beliefs, the change is accepted. Try to go in a direction counter to a self-limiting belief and your unconscious mind will burst forth with thoughts, feelings and behaviors that seem foreign and out of character. It will do whatever is necessary to corral you into a space that feels safe, comfortable, and supportive of your belief system.

I know. I've seen my own unconscious self at work and it wasn't pretty. One of my clearest memories of watching my unconscious emerge happened when I was working as a manager in a corporate setting. I don't remember exactly what pushed my buttons, but I do remember lashing out in a verbal attack on my boss in a departmental meeting. It was like watching a movie where someone else was using my mouth. Words and language I never use out loud flew from my lips as my anger boiled over. It was so out of character that my boss, who was also a therapist, began using techniques I recognized as those used to talk people off the Golden Gate Bridge. She was sure I was having a breakdown.

What my boss didn't know, and I didn't realize until much later, is that old negative beliefs were driving my unconscious mind into action. As a small child I was molested over a period of about 18 months by a babysitter and told to keep quiet or my family would be killed. I believed him and kept quiet for years. Later, shame would keep my mouth closed and I developed thoughts and feelings supporting the belief that I was a victim. Through the years, I developed habits of responding to threats and hurts with one of two extremes: retreating into silence or exploding in anger. The explosions were rare, and they frightened me when they happened.

My boss urged me to seek counseling and in those sessions I made the connection between my erratic behavior and my childhood pain. I continued in counseling for several years, and when that didn't seem to be working I tried just about anything I could to change my self-sabotaging habits. I studied Christian, Jewish, Buddhist, Hindu, and metaphysical teachings, psychology, fasting, healing prayer, and a host of techniques that all helped in various ways: but I still had my self-defeating problem. I loved and despised myself. I felt as if a big target had been put on my back aiming trouble my way. I wished that someone could take it off, and then I realized that the only person who could remove it was the one who had put it there. I finally recognized that I needed to transform the belief that I was a victim who had to hide or attack for survival. I needed to believe that I am resilient and whole. Creating the belief that I am resilient has enabled me to respond to challenging situations with reason and balance. I still get angry (usually at injustices and hurts, but without exploding), and my husband will tell you that I still tend to retreat when we butt heads, but I am no longer controlled by this unconscious self-limiting belief.

Shifting this one belief about resilience launched a journey that I continue to this day. I realized that I need to create healthy boundaries and meaningful connections. I learned that I can listen to my intuition and take meaningful action toward my goals. I discovered that I don't have to be a perfectionist to be excellent. I began to let go of a scarcity mentality and fear, and have welcomed abundance into my life. I now pursue my passions with the faith that I was designed by God to fulfill a purpose, and that I have been equipped with every resource necessary. **My mission is to share this message of hope with you that you can end self-sabotage and build better beliefs.**

Your Belief Quotient offers you a brief self-assessment to help you identify your old self-limiting beliefs. Based on research in cognitive behavior therapy, life and business coaching, and positive psychology as well as hundreds of interviews with clients and volunteers, *Your Belief Quotient* can help you identify and transform negative, self-sabotaging beliefs into beliefs that support and fuel your success.

In my research I found seven specific beliefs critical to creating a life of wholeness and balance. This book offers exercises to move you from victimization and defensiveness to **resilience**, isolation and dependence to **connectedness**, apathy and being consumed by activity to **initiative**, mediocrity and perfectionism to **excellence**, scarcity and entitlement to **abundance**, fear and ego to **faith**, and hopelessness and fanaticism to **purpose.** You will read a few of my clients' stories of transformation and change and as well as my personal experiences with breaking through belief barriers. Like us, you can consciously shift negative beliefs and move from sabotage to success.

I invite you to take the risk to examine your beliefs, work through the exercises and discover just how good life can be. Your unconscious mind can be like a cage with bars of self-limiting beliefs that keep all you are and all you can be just out of reach. Strengthening *Your Belief Quotient* is the key to unlocking the door to your success. **Freedom is waiting for you!**

CHAPTER 1

THE BEGINNINGS OF BELIEF

[bih-**leef**] An opinion or conviction.

"Man is what he believes."
Anton Chekhov

Imagine you are a pioneer traveling in a new land. No map exists for this strange place, but you are given a blank piece of paper to draw your own map as you travel down streets and roads. Every time you turn a corner or interact with one of the locals, you add to your map based on the information you gather. Your ability to understand the local language, culture and customs is limited, so your ability to create anything close to the truth is limited. Your perceptions are skewed because you do not have the whole picture. You assume you know where things are, but based on your incomplete knowledge and experience many of your assumptions are false. Distances and obstacles along your path are inaccurately minimized or magnified. You did the best you could, but you know the picture you have is lacking. Your map is flawed with false assumptions and misperceptions.

Your belief system is just like this map. Research has shown that unconscious beliefs are formed in early childhood, as early as age six. As a small child you started out with a very limited ability to understand the world around you, but you began collecting experiences. Each experience was added to your map in the form of a belief. Your beliefs were skewed by misperceptions and false assumptions as your childlike mind, will, and emotions sought to navigate through the world. Regardless of how distorted your map might be, it is the guide you will use for the rest of your life. Every new experience is measured against this map, every decision is based on the information you already have. The good news is **your map can be changed**!

Belief Systems

Your personal belief system plays a decisive role in how you view and create success. What is a belief system? Your belief system is a structured process by which you evaluate everything in your life. This process takes place beyond conscious thought, much like the operating system in a computer. Your operating system learns and adapts by taking in new information (perceptions) and ideas (assumptions). Over time you develop your own personal system of beliefs based on how you interpret the world around you. A belief system may start out much like a theory where assumptions are made based on logical observations and deductions. For example, you touch a hot stove for the first time and experience pain. You logically deduce that touching a stove again in the future, whether it is hot or not, could cause further pain. The skewed belief attached the concept of pain with the stove and not with the heat.

In other cases your belief may grow out of an emotional viewpoint that seems to be supported by logical assumptions. A mother snatches a small child back from the top of the stairs with a shriek to be careful not to fall. The child is frightened initially, not by the potential fall, but by the worry in his mother's voice. That fear is attached to the concept of falling and a leap in logic is transformed into the belief that all high places are to be feared. Children soak up the emotional responses of the adults around them as quickly as they do their own experiences.

When you consider how frequently you were warned, cautioned and disciplined as well as injured and harmed as a young child, it is not surprising that the majority (approximately 90%) of your thoughts and beliefs are negative. Unfortunately, this negative view of the world skews expectations for the rest of your life. To counter this negative view, you must develop the belief that you are resilient and able to survive and overcome any challenge or hardship. The importance of resilience and tools for increasing this belief are discussed in Chapter 3: Rebuilding Resilience.

Resistance to Changing Beliefs

Dr. F. H. Lund conducted experiments in the 1920s and found that "beliefs once formed are not willingly relinquished" and that the brain actually looks for evidence to support rather than challenge our beliefs.[1] This is called a "confirmation bias," when our minds seek confirmation rather than alternate views. As a small child, you attached certain beliefs to events. These assumptions were based on your limited knowledge of the world. Every other event that has occurred since that time has been interpreted through the lens of that existing belief. This would not be a problem if every belief you created supported your health and well-being, but some of the beliefs you formed were inaccurate and even destructive.

Beliefs are also influenced by our environment. Over time, messages we hear over and over again begin to take root in our minds. The television shows you watch, the papers you read, the friends you spend time with, and the music you listen to all influence your beliefs. Take a young person with very strong beliefs and place him in a new setting where those beliefs are subtly challenged day after day, and his beliefs will begin to shift. **There is a natural desire in all of us to conform to the beliefs and behaviors of those around us.**

In the 1950s social psychologist Solomon Asch created experiments that tested conformity.[2] In his experiments a group of people would intentionally select an incorrect response in front of the test subject. The subject was not aware that all the others had been coached on their responses. When asked to respond after hearing the other members of the group, the subject would begin to question his own perceptions and agree with the answer selected by the others. The subject's beliefs were challenged and even shifted by the influence of the group. Asch was disturbed by these results: On a personal level, if you are spending your time surrounded by individuals who are influenced by negative, self-limiting beliefs, you are at risk of having your healthy beliefs erode and conform to the beliefs of your companions. **Unconscious self-limiting beliefs can be contagious.**

Once your beliefs have been formed, your brain looks for evidence to support them. When you are confronted with clear evidence that your belief is incorrect, your conscious mind may accept the evidence and act on it, but your unconscious mind resists and undermines your attempts to change. For example, a child who was bitten by a dog may grow up with the belief that all dogs are bad. As an adult they know on a conscious level that not all dogs are bad or going to bite, but the unconscious mind clings to the belief. The unconscious mind can create a sense of discomfort, a phobia, or even an allergy to dogs in order to protect the belief that dogs are bad. In another example, a child who was yelled at and told he was stupid by his parents might grow up to believe he is incompetent and unable to achieve any standard of excellence regardless of how well he performs at school or work. Unconsciously his mind finds support for his belief and will even twist positive experiences into evidence that he is worthless.

At first your beliefs are soft and flexible, subject to change based on new information. Over time your beliefs become stronger, less flexible and well entrenched in your mind. Once established, beliefs are accepted as fact and are rarely subject to scrutiny. Your brain is wired to protect your map, or your unconscious belief system. Every time you are presented with evidence that does not fit with what is on the map, the brain rejects the new information in favor of the old belief. Even when a faulty belief is exposed on a conscious level, the brain will find ways to reinforce and support that belief in your unconscious mind. Your mind sees protection of your belief system as vital to your survival. This explains why a person determined to change a habit ends up defeated so often. If that habit is tied to an old belief, your unconscious mind will create opportunities to self-sabotage and undermine your success.

This resistance to change can show up in many forms. The first way your mind protects your beliefs is through denial. You generally go through life oblivious of your unconscious beliefs. Occasionally beliefs will be recognized, and your first reaction is to deny its existence. When faced with the possibility that you hold a negative belief, you begin looking for evidence that you do not hold that belief. The greatest tool of evil in the world is deception: the belief in something that is not true. Self-deception is buying into lies and reinforcing them to protect faulty beliefs. Another tactic used by your mind to protect your beliefs is negative emotion. When faced with the truth, many people feel depressed, anxious or angry. Then when attempting to change that belief, the emotions increase in intensity. It is not uncommon for someone to feel panicked when they begin to attempt to change. The first sign that change will not come easily can trigger a sense of hopelessness. If the process of change is being guided by someone else, feelings of intense anger and even rage can be directed toward that person. These emotions are not based on logic or fact. They are tools your unconscious mind uses to protect your belief system. Understanding how the brain works will help you understand how to uncover and shift your beliefs to a more positive, supportive system.

> *"The brain is a world consisting of a number of unexplored continents and great stretches of unknown territory."*
>
> *Santiago Ramon y Cajal*

Beliefs and the Brain

The brain is an amazing organ made up of three sections: the brain stem, the cortex, and the limbic system. The brain stem is the part of your brain responsible for survival and is well protected in the deepest part of your brain, connecting to the spinal cord. The focus of the brain stem is to maintain functions like breathing and blood flow. This area of the brain also serves as a relay station for information to and from other areas of the brain. Conscious thought is not formulated in the brain stem, but sensations required for survival, including instinct, are generated here.

The limbic system is located in the center of the brain and is responsible for housing your emotions, appetites and motivation. Where the brain stem promotes routine and ritualized behavior, the limbic system creates passion, emotion and the desire for change. Dr. Daniel Amen is a psychiatrist known for his work using SPECT (specific positron emission computer tomography) scans to identify areas where the brain is not functioning optimally.[3] In his book *Change Your Brain, Change Your Life*, Dr. Amen describes the consequences of an under-active or over-active limbic system:

> The emotional shading provided by the deep limbic system is the filter through which you interpret the events of the day. It colors events depending on your emotional state of mind. When you are sad (with an overactive deep limbic system), you are likely to interpret neutral events through a negative filter. For example, if you have a neutral or even positive conversation with someone whose deep limbic system is overactive or "negatively set," he or she is likely to interpret the conversation in a negative way. When this part of the brain is "cool" or functions properly, a neutral or positive interpretation of events is more likely to occur.[4]

Together the brain stem and the limbic system organize sensory input and responses. This data is then communicated to the top layer of the brain called the cortex. The cortex is only about one quarter of an inch thick, but it is densely populated with neurons. Neurons are the cells in your brain responsible for communication. There are approximately 100 billion neurons in the human brain, and the vast majority of them are in the cerebral cortex. The cortex is responsible for what is known as higher cognitive function. Your ability to learn and solve problems, think critically, remember, express thought and emotion, recognize communication, appreciate music, focus and shift your attention, control impulses, cooperate and adapt resides in the cerebral cortex.

Every time you learn or experience something, a rush of chemicals is stimulated in the brain. These chemicals, called neurotransmitters, trigger responses based on where these bursts are located in the brain.

Information from one neuron flows to another neuron across an appendage called a synapse. Neurons communicate back and forth as electrical charges pulse rapidly through the synapse, causing neurotransmitters to be produced and collected by other synapses. Every time a neural pathway is used, the connection of those neurons is strengthened. When a pathway is rarely used, the connection weakens and eventually dies. This process is called synaptic pruning.

As fascinating and mysterious as it might seem, the brain is nothing more than an organ. Like the liver or kidneys or heart, it is not capable of changing itself. However, **the brain is changed chemically by beliefs, thoughts, feelings and behaviors produced by the mind.** Every time a synapse fires information from one neuron to another, the brain shifts and changes. The mind is the product of the brain. It is the brain at work. Because of the billions of neurons active in your brain, you have an infinite potential of creating different kinds of minds, perspectives or beliefs. All those neurons process about 400 billion bits of information per second, but you are only aware of approximately 2000 bits of that information. Your awareness extends only toward your body, your environment and time. You think about whether you are hot or cold, whether the chair you are sitting in is comfortable, and just how long is this chapter going to be? Your mind is bombarded by thought after thought. But even with all of the thoughts whirling around in your head, you are missing most of what is going on—unless you make a conscious effort to slow down and pay attention. The exercises at the end of each chapter are designed to help you become more aware of your conscious and unconscious mind. Awareness of your beliefs will allow you to consciously choose to strengthen neural pathways that support your success. You can change your mind and your brain by changing your beliefs, and that will change your life.

Positivity, Personality, and Beliefs

Why does change seem to come more easily for some people than for others? There are many possible reasons. You tend to inherit certain patterns of brain behavior from your family such as a tendency toward anxiety or hyperactivity. Early childhood trauma can create a series of beliefs that are more resistant to change. Martin Seligman's research on "learned helplessness" found that the majority of individuals who were confronted with conditions beyond their control collapsed physically, emotionally, and spiritually. Seligman's work in this field led him to question just what it is that allows us to bounce back and not become helpless. This was a new concept in the 1990s after decades of psychoanalytic approaches that focused solely on minimizing suffering rather than increasing resilience and well-being.[5] Seligman is considered the Father of Positive Psychology, and research in this field is demonstrating that behavioral change is possible by replacing helplessness with resilience.[6]

Dr. Barbara Frederickson is conducting solid research in the field of positivity. She defines positivity as the experience of positive emotions including love, joy, interest, gratitude, and hope.[7] Until recently, these concepts and their effects have been a mystery to science. But Dr. Frederickson contends that "these are not just words, but are deeply heart felt and change our mind's chemistry." In her book *Positivity*, Dr. Frederickson's research reveals that emotions obey a tipping point. Experiencing three or more positive emotions for every negative emotion will cause you to flourish.[8] Sustained behavioral change is possible when positive emotions (accompanied by unconscious incentives and increased resources) generate passion for the new behavior. Exercises based on Dr. Frederickson's model will help you create the change that may have been eluding you.

Basic differences in human personality might also give one person a stronger preference for familiarity and sameness where another prefers flexibility, spontaneity and change. The *Myers-Briggs Type Indicator*® categorizes personality traits into four basic temperaments and expands these four into 16 unique personality types. These types are based on the preferences of each, whether someone is more energized by being around others (Extraversion) or by being alone (Introversion); whether they gather information concretely through the senses (Sensing) or prefer theory and abstract thought (iNtuitive); whether they make judgments based on logic (Thinking) or emotion (Feeling); and whether they prefer structure and order (Judging) or spontaneity and flexibility (Perceiving).[9] Even though each person has a basic temperament and overall type, none of the traits described above are set in stone. Individuals taking the Myers-Briggs will see their scores shift somewhat at different times because of life circumstances. Someone who is more likely to make decisions based on logic can develop the ability to empathize and consider emotion before making a judgment. An individual who prefers structure, timelines, and order can develop the ability to be more flexible. Personality type is not an excuse to resist change when change is needed. Some of the exercises in this book were designed with personality type in mind to help you create the change you want.

Characteristics of a Healthy Belief System

Imagine that you have the chance to build your dream home. In this perfect picture you have imagined the front of the house with trees and flowers and a path to the door. You know the floor plan and have already begun decorating your beautiful home in your mind. But what if the house was not built properly? What if the floor couldn't handle the weight of anyone walking across and it collapsed beneath you? What if you found you had no walls between the TV room and the baby's bedroom? What if you discovered clogged pipes were installed and the water couldn't flow through the plumbing? Or what if you tried to turn on the lights and the garage door opened instead? Your beautiful dream would become a nightmare of hazards and repairs. Just as there are important steps to building a house, there are keys to creating a healthy belief system.

Every house needs a firm foundation that can handle the weight of the building. A building foundation is created by laying supports that go deeper and wider than the actual building. The foundation keeps the building standing when storms or an earthquake could shake it apart. Just like houses, your belief system needs a foundation. Resilience is the ability to recover and hold up under the stresses of illness, change, or misfortune. **Holding the belief that you are resilient and *not* a victim to your past or present circumstances is the foundation to your success.**

Once a foundation is laid and the supports are built, contractors are able to build the walls of a home. Walls identify space and establish boundaries between one room and the next. Without walls you wouldn't be able to tell one room from another. The electrical wiring of a house is usually placed within the walls and allows you to be able to flip a switch and have the lights turn on or the garbage disposal run. The walls and wiring of a home give us a picture of how each of us needs to feel connected to others in healthy ways. **The belief that you are a separate, unique individual connected to others in meaningful relationships is important to your well-being.**

The walls of a house create useful barriers, but windows are important to let in light and fresh air. Windows can be blocked with opaque glass, draperies or dirt. The clearer the window, the more light will be able to fill the rooms. When those windows are stuck closed, the air stops moving and gets stale. Openness is the quality of being willing to receive abundance, consider new and different ideas, and accept new methods or opportunities. Openness to abundance is like shining new light into your thinking. **Individuals who have an abundance mindset are ready to receive the blessings and joys coming their way.**

The flow of water through your house is the benefit of a good plumbing system. The ability to turn a knob and have a cool, fresh drink of water or a hot, steamy shower is something most of us expect in our homes. Clear pipes and valves allow water to move through your home. A clog in one of those pipes can block the flow and keep the water from being delivered to your sink or bathtub. The belief that you can take and maintain initiative creates a flow in your life similar to the flow of water. This flow creates momentum and gets things done. Without initiative, you become stuck, and the flow of effort or ideas is blocked. **Creating a strong sense of personal initiative will allow you to get things moving in your life.**

As construction on your house continues, you will need to have it inspected to make sure that it meets building codes and standards. Building codes measure whether or not a building has been crafted with excellence. An inspector can save you from a lot of grief by identifying poor work. At the same time, inspectors have to be balanced with realistic expectations. You don't want an inspector holding up work on your house by picking everything apart and expecting perfection. Your beliefs around personal standards undermine or support your success. Whether or not you believe you can expect excellence from yourself determines what you can and will achieve. Overly high standards can create the paralysis of perfectionism. **Shifting your belief to a balanced expectation of excellence transforms the outcome of everything you do.**

Many modern buildings include a skylight in the roof. Skylights are special types of windows that serve to open a ceiling to a view of the sky beyond. Research has shown that the belief that there is a Higher Power, Source, or Creator is very supportive to growth and change. This characteristic of belief is faith, the sense that there is something more beyond yourself. This belief calls for deep sense of humility. **Having faith in an abundant universe that conspires for your good is a belief held by the most successful people in the world.**

Once your beautiful home has been built, you can either move in or choose to leave it vacant. It seems ridiculous to go to the effort of building a beautiful home, only to leave it empty. You would be ignoring the purpose for which it was built. Many people live their lives day after day without any thought of intention or purpose. Connecting to the belief that your life has meaning and purpose is perhaps the most powerful thing you can do. **Studies show measurable results, better outcomes, more passion and greater joy in every area of life when people find and seek to fulfill their purpose.**

Your Belief Quotient offers you the opportunity to examine these seven characteristics of a healthy belief system: resilience, connectedness, abundance, initiative, excellence, faith and purpose. Each chapter offers exercises and activities that will strengthen these areas. Unlike building a house where you have to construct the foundation before the walls, you can work on building these beliefs in any order. You can choose to focus on strengthening beliefs that are already strong or building better beliefs in areas that are weak. *Your Belief Quotient* will change as your perceptions and attitudes toward yourself change. Create the intention of building better beliefs and focus your attention on opportunities to exercise new habits, and you will see your life transformed. You will be building the life you barely dreamed was possible.

Why These Seven Beliefs?

The seven beliefs in the Belief Quotient assessment were not chosen randomly. The research behind this tool goes back several decades. Bear with me as I explain the background for this process.

Psychologist Alfred Adler is known for creating the term "inferiority complex" and studying negative beliefs. Adler developed a system designed to take people from a sense of inferiority to superiority. He believed that there are five basic mistaken and self-defeating perceptions (see chart below). As research for this book was done, seven beliefs emerged as being crucial to success. Five of these beliefs relate closely to Adler's list. In the chart on the next page you will find Adler's five self-defeating perceptions, their definitions, and the seven supportive beliefs that make up *Your Belief Quotient*.

Adler's 5 Self-Defeating Perceptions	Adler's Definitions	7 Characteristics of a Healthy Belief Quotient	Definitions
Overgeneralization	The belief that there is no fairness in the world.	Resilience	The belief that I can succeed and prosper even after facing setbacks and hardships.

Adler's 5 Self-Defeating Perceptions	Adler's Definitions	7 Characteristics of a Healthy Belief Quotient	Definitions
False or impossible goals of security	The belief that I must please everyone if I am to feel loved.	Connectedness	The belief that I am connected to others in meaningful relationships.
Misperceptions of life and life's demands	The belief that life is too hard.	Initiative	The belief that I can begin to take action and follow through with determination.
Minimization or denial of one's worth	The belief that I am basically stupid.	Excellence	The belief that I am worthy and able to live up to high standards I create for myself.
Faulty values	The belief that I must get to the top regardless of who gets hurt in the process.	Purpose	The belief that my life has meaning, value, a calling.
		Abundance	The belief that there is plenty, and that good is coming my way.
		Faith	The belief that there is something beyond myself, a Higher Power at work in me and the world.

Raising Your Belief Quotient

Adler described overgeneralization as the view that the world is unfair and unsafe. These feelings spring from wounds and traumas of the past and create a victim mentality. Shifting from victimization to resilience strengthens self-esteem and instills hope that a better future is possible. Adler defined false or impossible goals of security as the belief that you must please everyone if you are to feel loved. This belief is highly destructive as the sensation grows that you can never be good enough or lovable enough. It creates a sense of isolation and disconnection from self, others and God. Creating meaningful connections is essential to wholeness.

Adler described misperceptions of life and life's demands as the belief that life is too hard. Individuals suffering with this belief quit before they try and fall into a heap of failure and apathy. Learning to take initiative and believing in your ability to maintain certain acts of discipline strengthens your resolve to try until you find success. In addition to believing they lack the resolve to take action, many people believe they lack the intelligence to succeed. Adler called this minimization or denial of one's worth. When you believe you don't have what it takes to succeed, you may find yourself accepting mediocrity as a way of life instead of creating and believing in standards of excellence.

According to Adler, faulty values were the root cause of the belief that you must get to the top regardless of who gets hurt in the process. This approach to life can be mildly self-centered or extreme to the point of being sociopathic. Discovering your true calling or life's purpose brings great joy to yourself and others. It is founded on beliefs that support your success and builds up others in the process.[10]

Two additional beliefs are addressed in *Your Belief Quotient.* One characteristic belief is abundance. A healthy belief system will be based on an abundance mentality that there is more than enough. Scarcity thinking, closed-mindedness and intolerance are destructive and self-limiting. Entitlement is equally destructive. An abundant mindset is open to others, willing to exchange ideas and resources. Your beliefs need input from others to be challenged to grow. The more secure you are in your sense of self and your beliefs, the more willing you will be to consider differing opinions and ideas. This does not mean blind acceptance, but a willingness to consider the possibility of new beliefs.

Another belief essential to success is faith. This belief is not based in religion. It is the belief that there is a Higher Power at work, loving you, conspiring for your good, and providing every resource necessary. It is essential to success. The opposite of this belief is fear. Moving from fear to faith makes movement toward the other positive beliefs possible. Research into the benefits of this belief has recently moved from metaphysics to hard science as the effects of faith has been measured in the brain and the body. In studies of spontaneous remission of disease observed by Dr. Joe Dispenza (a chiropractor, neuroscience researcher and author of *Evolve Your Brain*), every person who recovered from disease in this study described a belief in an intelligence within themselves giving them life. They believed they had a connection to a Mind greater than the self, a Mind who loved them more than they loved themselves—enough to give them life. Dispenza quotes one patient from the study as saying, "I'm riding on the back of a Giant and I just need to learn to whisper in its ear."[11] This conscious awareness and reliance on Something Other than yourself is faith.

Each of the seven characteristics of a healthy belief system can be seen as a continuum moving from unhealthy to healthy attitudes as demonstrated on the chart on the next page:

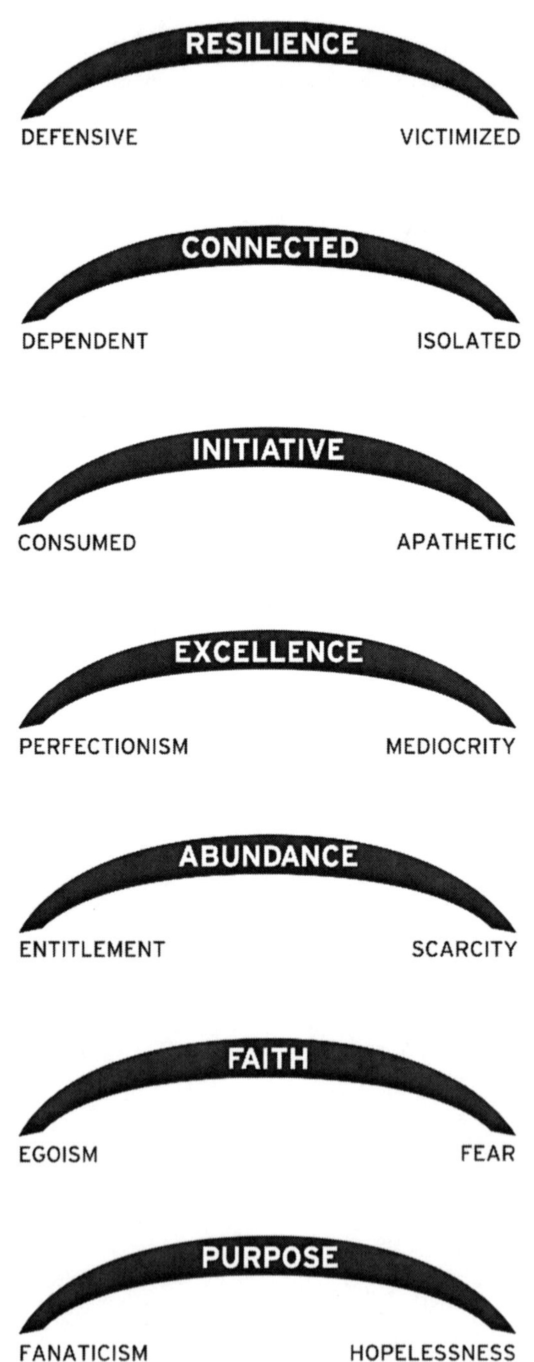
RESILIENCE
DEFENSIVE
VICTIMIZED
CONNECTED
DEPENDENT
ISOLATED
INITIATIVE
CONSUMED
APATHETIC
EXCELLENCE
PERFECTIONISM
MEDIOCRITY
ABUNDANCE
ENTITLEMENT
SCARCITY
FAITH
EGOISM
FEAR
PURPOSE
FANATICISM
HOPELESSNESS

Many therapeutic models including family therapy, cognitive behavior therapy, and ratio-emotive therapy are founded on the process developed by Albert Adler. His process is also similar to life coaching as the client is considered misguided rather than sick. The client and therapist are seen as collaborators in the process of shifting self-defeating perceptions. In order to shift these beliefs, Adler used a variety of tools and techniques to increase awareness, acceptance, practice and reinforcement of new beliefs. Martin Seligman more recently has suggested that the path to well-being consists of 1) Positive Emotions, 2) Engagement / flow, 3) Relationships / social connections, 4) Meaning / purpose, 5) Accomplishment. Positive psychology offers strong support as we look at building better beliefs in each of these areas.[12]

Building Better Beliefs

Your Belief Quotient uses tools adapted from the fields of psychotherapy, counseling and coaching. You begin by identifying your unconscious negative beliefs. In Chapter 2 you will find a brief assessment on which you will rate yourself on certain behaviors, feelings, thoughts and beliefs. The questions target your beliefs in the seven key areas described above. Recognizing where your belief system might be weak is vital to being able to create new, supportive beliefs. You can't fix something that you are unaware is broken.

You also cannot fix something if you refuse to accept the need for change. As described earlier in this chapter, your unconscious mind is going to fight change. It is possible that you will react to some of the questions and the results of the assessment. You might question the validity of the tool or the motives of the author. You might decide that you were in a bad mood and selected responses that don't accurately reflect your beliefs. You might become angry and toss this book in the garbage. Each of these responses demonstrates an unconscious mind fighting to survive. Push through the denial and negative emotions, accept that you have specific weaknesses in your belief system, and surrender to the concept that you have work to do.

Once you have identified the beliefs that need to be shifted in order for you to be more successful, work through the exercises at the end of each chapter. These exercises are designed to build your awareness of your beliefs. When you become more conscious of the beliefs behind your thoughts, feelings and behavior, it will become easier to shift the belief. The exercises will provide opportunities to practice new skills and reinforce new beliefs. You cannot destroy negative beliefs without replacing them with positive, supportive beliefs.

Another way of looking at this process is to use the word POWER as an acronym. This is a tool I have used with children as young as age six and adults in their 70s. To have or set an intention is: "to have in mind a purpose or plan, to direct the mind, to aim." Lacking intention, we sometimes wander without meaning or direction, or worse, fall into negative thinking patterns and behavior. You can transform your life by using the following method to set intentions and take inspired action toward shifting your belief system.

P — What is the **problem** I am facing? Am I clear about what I want to shift?

Janet Attwood, author of *The Passion Test* says that you can have anything you want but only to the extent you are clear.[13] Briefly, getting clear is eliminating negative thoughts and freeing your mind to be open to possibilities and opportunities. Once you've set aside your emotional blocks, you are able to see past them to the bright hopes you have for yourself. There is nothing wrong with wanting more. Writing down your intentions activates your unconscious mind and engages your body, mind and spirit in a process that seeks to fulfill your expectation. According to a study done by Dominican University, people who write down their intentions, goals and objectives achieve 90% more than those who don't.

O — What are my **options**? Is surrender necessary, or can I continue on as I am? How are these beliefs showing up in my day-to-day life?

Generating options is vital to goal achievement and the fulfillment of your intention. When you engage in brainstorming and opening your mind to possibilities, you become a creative problem solver. Your unconscious mind begins to search for the resources necessary to achieve your goal. You begin to attract solutions *before you even begin to take action*! Generating options pulls you out of rigid, programmed thinking, making it easier to move away from negative patterns toward proactive, positive paths. Young children usually are very good at generating options as they are not as programmed to find the "right" answer. Playfully generating outrageous options in a childlike manner can be a healthy way to shift your beliefs and your behavior.

W — How will I **work** on and practice my new skills? What specifically am I going to do to create change?

One simple step will take you toward your goal. Inaction is not neutral. It is actually a step away from your goal of creating a healthy belief system. Choose one simple step and build confidence before you take another. Stretch yourself with every success, and then venture out into taking strategic risks and challenges. Forward motion is the best indicator of a commitment to achieve your goals. Sharing your intention with someone you trust is an important step as it reinforces your commitment to that dream and the action steps it will take to achieve it. Be sure to share your dream with someone worthy of carrying it with you. They should have the same values and ideals you have. They should be supportive and objective. They should only hold you accountable for the actions you wish to commit to and not insert their opinions or ideas. Accountability is a catalyst for growth and change, but it frequently carries a negative connotation because it has been misused in a controlling or manipulative manner. Make sure that you have the support and encouragement to succeed.

E — How will I know I am improving? How will I **evaluate** my progress?

Ask for feedback from an accountability partner and others who know you well. Assess whether you completed the action step as well as you could and whether you are ready for the next step. Measure your progress and acknowledge forward motion. If course corrections are necessary, make them early to prevent yourself from drifting further and further from your intention.

R — What will I do to **reinforce** my progress and **reward** my success?

Celebrate your successes! Your reward might be a simple "WooHoo!" on Facebook or something more substantial, but patting yourself on the back is an important part of fulfilling your intentions. Your unconscious mind needs positive feedback that it has successfully directed you toward your goal in order to be ready to take on the next challenge. Enjoy your progress . . . and then **REPEAT** the process with the next action step until you see your new beliefs manifested.

Put **POWER** to work for you as you complete the Belief Quotient assessment and the exercises. Using this tool will enable you to overcome resistance and create forward momentum as you begin to rewrite your childhood map, put your brain to work, and raise *Your Belief Quotient.*

CHAPTER 2

YOUR BELIEF QUOTIENT

"If you secretly don't believe in yourself . . . you will secretly sabotage your success. Eliminate self-doubt, fears and any feeling of being less than or not good enough and rise to the fact that you were born to achieve the seeds of greatness within your genes. Today is your day, seize it and become all you are meant to become. Wait no more, do it now!"
John Assaraf

Raising *Your Belief Quotient* is hard work. The process is going to make you uncomfortable, but you know that the effort is worth it. You are tired of living a diminished life, and even more tired of getting in your own way. You could compare the process to peeling back layers of an onion or scrubbing away inches of muck. Peeling onions can make you cry, and there could be tears in this process. Scrubbing muck requires that you get your hands dirty and expose yourself to stuff you find repelling. That might be true here as well. But I can't think of an analogy that will prepare you for the resistance your unconscious mind is going to create when you begin to attack your self-sabotaging beliefs.

Self-sabotaging beliefs reside deep in the unconscious mind. Because of this it can be difficult to identify these beliefs and eradicate them. Your unconscious mind is uncomfortable and even resistant to change. Creating a relaxed state of mind where you can flow in a stream of consciousness will help you locate your beliefs. How do you do this? First, you will want to be in a quiet place where all distractions have been eliminated. You will need a series of questions that you haven't seen or spent time with so your unconscious mind hasn't had a chance to prepare "acceptable answers". These questions could be on a page you haven't looked at before or they could be presented to you by someone you trust.

This chapter offers two sets of questions designed to help you to identify your unconscious beliefs and then a section on how to change self-limiting beliefs. The first section contains a series of **Self-Reflection Questions**. These questions are open-ended statements that offer you the opportunity to capture the first thing that comes to mind. As suggested above, it might benefit you to have an objective person like a coach or mentor ask these questions and write your responses so you can stay relaxed and open. You want to capture the first thoughts that come to mind. Your responses will expose patterns of beliefs and the areas where your self-sabotaging beliefs live. These areas correspond to the beliefs covered in the second section: the Belief Quotient Assessment.

Before taking the **Belief Quotient Assessment**, you will want to make sure you are in a relaxed state of mind. Focus on your life as a whole where indicated, and on your recent past (the last six months) when asked about your attitudes and actions now. Avoid trying to select a "correct" response, but instead select the response that is closest to how you truly perceive yourself.

Once you have your results from the Belief Quotient Assessment, I recommend you reread your responses to the Self-Reflection Questions. With both of these tools in mind, then move to the third part of this chapter: **Changing Your Beliefs**. This section contains the specific steps required to shift your negative beliefs.

Self-Reflection Questions

Take a few minutes now and consider the self-reflection questions below. For best results, have a trusted coach or mentor read the statements aloud to you and record your responses. Write or say the first thing that comes to your mind:

- I am . . . .
- I am not . . .

- I am good with . . .
- I am not good with . . .
- I will never be able to . . .
- I don't deserve . . .
- I am held back by . . .
- Other people . . .
- Men are . . .
- Women are . . .
- Money is . . .
- God is . . .
- I always . . .
- I never . . .
- I should . . .
- I have to . . .
- I want . . .
- Where am I holding myself back?
- Which of my strengths/abilities could I be using more?
- What could I achieve if I really believed in myself?

Completing the statements above can help identify negative patterns and beliefs. This exercise is particularly powerful when you focus on a specific area or event in your life. Discussing your statements with a trusted mentor or coach can help you get even more clarity on beliefs that are not serving you.

Development of the Belief Quotient Assessment

The Belief Quotient Assessment was designed to provide a measurement of one's belief system. As the assessment evolved, seven specific beliefs were identified as being particularly important to one's success: resilience, connectedness, initiative, excellence, abundance, faith and purpose. Each of these beliefs is represented by a continuum, with a skewed and a weakened belief at either end and the balanced, healthy belief in the center. The assessment asks a series of questions relating to each belief. By selecting the response that best describes how you see yourself, you will be able to get an objective measure of your beliefs.

The Belief Quotient assessment was tested on over 200 people before going to print. Most of those who helped test the Belief Quotient were professionals from a wide variety of industries as well as business owners and entrepreneurs.

As with all assessments, results can be affected by a number of factors: your circumstances, mood, physical health and whether you truly want accurate results or not. Your Belief Quotient is not a number set in stone. You can change your Belief Quotient and create a system of beliefs that ensure your success.

Discover Your Belief Quotient

Rate yourself on the following statements by circling the number of points for the response that matches your attitudes and actions best. Add up your points at the end each section for a Subtotal score.

Please note: You will benefit the most from this process and the rest of the book by being as honest as you can in your responses.

1. When I think about the past . . .

   1 - I avoid thinking about the past because it makes me tense and angry.
   5 - I feel mostly warm and happy.
   10 - I feel mostly sad, ashamed and/or afraid.

2. When I make a mistake . . .

   1 - I tend to blame someone or something for causing it.
   5 - I tend to face up to it and move forward.
   10 - I tend to try to cover it up.

3. When I set out to accomplish something . . .

    1 - I tend to run into frustrating roadblocks and delays.
    5 - I tend to get it done with a little effort.
    10 - I tend to fall apart and need help getting things done.

4. When I try something new or different . . .

    1 - I don't want anyone watching me look foolish.
    5 - I can laugh at my own awkwardness.
    10 - I don't try new things very often because it's just too hard.

5. When it comes to my health . . .

    1 - I don't like people pushing vitamins or cures at me.
    5 - I take pretty good care of myself and only get sick occasionally.
    10 - I have a lot of headaches, aches and pains and feel tired.

6. When I think about strengths or talents . . .

    1 - I know I'm not the best in the world, but I do what I can.
    5 - I enjoy using my specific strengths and talents and am thankful for them.
    10 - I am not really sure I have any specific strengths or talents.

7. When I make decisions or choices . . .

   1 - I don't need any input from anyone else. I want to stand on my own two feet.
   5 - I am willing to listen to others, but make the final decision based on what I want and believe is right.
   10 - I need someone to outline the best options and tell me what to do.

Subtotal A _______________

8. When I am discouraged, in pain or stuck . . .

   1 - I tend to talk to everyone I know about it.
   5 - I tend to reach out to close friends or family for help.
   10 - I tend to work things out on my own.

9. When people around me are emotional . . .

   1 - I am strongly affected.
   5 - I am moved by their emotions.
   10 - I am not affected.

10. When someone else is talking about something important to them . . .

   1 - I listen for awhile and then share what is going on with me.
   5 - I listen and ask open-ended questions.
   10 - I don't like to listen to people drone on about themselves.

11. When a friend or family member wants something from me . . .

    1 - I have a hard time saying no, even if it means sacrificing myself.
    5 - I am able to say no if its something I don't think would be good for me.
    10 - People don't usually ask me for anything because they know I'll say no.

12. When I need something . . .

    1 - I have a hard time finding help because I've already asked for too many favors.
    5 - I have several friends or family members I can go to for help.
    10 - I wouldn't ask, but wish someone would notice and offer to help.

13. When it comes to a sense of spirituality . . .

    1 - I rely on religious leaders to guide me.
    5 - I have a deep personal faith and spirituality.
    10 - I don't know or don't believe in a Higher Power beyond myself.

14. When there is drama in my relationships with friends and family . . .

    1 - I am right in the middle of it to the point of exhaustion.
    5 - I am involved only if I'm part of the solution and can pull away to take care of myself when necessary.
    10 - I don't get involved.

Subtotal B ________________

15. When there is a new project . . .

    1 - I jump right in and work on it until its completed perfectly.
    5 - I ask pertinent questions, work hard, and take breaks when I need them.
    10 - I do what I am asked to do as best as I can.

16. When a new project is beginning . . .

    1 - I am the first in the door and the last to leave so I can get it all done.
    5 - I am excited to get to work on new projects and balance them with current commitments.
    10 - I feel like I already have a lot to do.

17. When it comes to taking risks to achieve my goals . . .

    1 - I will do whatever it takes, nothing will get in my way.
    5 - I will take calculated risks.
    10 - I don't think taking risks is necessary.

18. When things get tough . . .

    1 - I push through to get things done perfectly no matter what it takes.
    5 - I do all I can and do it well.
    10 - I take a break and let someone else take their turn.

19. When it comes to discipline . . .

    1 - I am habit-driven because I need to be the best at everything I do.

5 - I have activities that I follow through regularly that make me successful in my niche.
10 - I have very little will-power and follow through—it's just hard work.

20. When I need to focus . . .

1 - I have trouble shifting my focus once I get started.
5 - I can focus on something for a while and then need a break.
10 - I have trouble concentrating.

21. When I take breaks . . .

1 - I feel guilty and think about work the whole time.
5 - I do something fun or relaxing and then get back to work.
10 - I take as long as I can and drag my feet going back to work.

Subtotal C ______________

22. When I look at the quality of my work . . .

1 - I usually am not satisfied—nothing is ever "good enough."
5 - I usually feel good about what I accomplish. I do good work.
10 - I know I could do better if I worked a little harder, but it's good enough.

23. When it comes to following up on details . . .

    1 - I usually have multiple systems for monitoring and check details frequently.
    5 - I generally am proactive and intentional about checking up on things.
    10 - I rarely go back and check on things after I've looked at it once.

24. When it comes to organization . . .

    1 - I usually have tracking systems and systems to back up my systems.
    5 - I generally am organized and pay attention to details on projects.
    10 - I'm not the most organized and tend to regularly lose track of things.

25. When it comes to success . . .

    1 - Success is something I strive for every breathing moment.
    5 - Success is something I plan and pursue.
    10 - Success is something I hope will happen for me.

26. When it comes to my things . . .

    1 - I am meticulous in how I care for my home, car, clothing, etc.
    5 - I am responsible in how I care for my home, car, clothing, etc.
    10 - I am lazy in how I care for my home, car, clothing, etc.

27. When it comes to spontaneity and flexibility . . .

1 - I prefer to have everything planned ahead well in advance and to have everything go as planned.
5 - I prefer to have a plan that leaves room for some flexibility.
10 - I prefer to leave the planning to others and go with the flow.

28. When it comes to personal standards of excellence . . .

1 - I expect myself to get it right the first time and be the best every time.
5 - I expect myself to do well every time and get a little better every time.
10 - I expect I will get it done when its done and hope it isn't any harder next time.

Subtotal D ______________

29. When I am paid money for my work . . .

1 - I am rarely paid what I am worth. I should be getting a lot more.
5 - I am usually paid fairly for the work I do. I am thankful for my paycheck.
10 - I am always worried it will not be enough. I need to make more.

30. When I think about my health . . .

1 - I should be getting better care from my providers. They don't treat me like a priority.

5 - I am responsible for my health and healthcare decisions and make choices that lead to good health.
10 - I wish I felt better, but I always seem to be sick.

31. When I think of a Higher Power (God/the Universe) outside of myself . . .

1 - I expect things to go well because that's what happens to good people like me.
5 - I believe God/the Universe conspires for my good and blesses me whether I deserve it or not.
10 - I hope I haven't offended God/the Universe too much if there is such a thing.

32. When it comes to time . . .

1 - Even if I waste time, things will work out for me.
5 - There is always enough time when I am responsible.
10 - There is never enough time.

33. When I look at how things move through my life . . .

1 - I expect things to go well because they just should.
5 - I know how to get out of my own way and enjoy the flow of synchronicity.
10 - I feel like things are chaotic and out of control.

34. When I am with a group of people . . .

    1 - I want more time and attention on me.
    5 - I enjoy the flow of giving and receiving.
    10 - I don't think people even notice me.

35. When I look at the future . . .

    1 - I deserve to have it all.
    5 - Good things are coming my way.
    10 - I hope things are better than they are now.

Subtotal E _______________

36. When I think about God / a Higher Power beyond myself . . .

    1 - I believe I make my own luck.
    5 - I believe in God / a Higher Power beyond myself.
    10 - I am afraid and uncertain.

37. When I think about the unknown future ahead . . .

    1 - I'm working to make sure everything is going to work out the way I want it to.
    5 - I believe everything is going to be just fine because God/My Higher Power has everything under control.
    10 - Fear of the unknown paralyzes me.

38. When life is uncertain . . .

    1 - I charge ahead and make things happen.

5 - I move ahead anyway and thoughtfully / prayerfully make leaps of faith necessary to grow.

10 - I feel paralyzed and stop moving forward.

39. When it comes to absolutes and standards . . .

1 - I follow my own code and don't care what anyone thinks.

5 - I follow a set of absolute principles that govern my character and actions.

10 - I do think we should stay out of each other's business and not offend.

40. When my personal standards conflict with someone else's behavior . . .

1 - I believe anyone who doesn't think like I do is wrong.

5 - I believe love is the best way to resolve differences and will draw all of us closer to Absolute Truth.

10 - I believe my standards should be flexible and non-judgmental.

41. When bad things happen . . .

1 - I am angry and question why is this happening in my world.

5 - I am hopeful and have internal resources that help me trust things will work out, even if that means working out differently than I expected.

10 - I am depressed and worry what will happen next.

42. When I don't see how things could possibly work out . . .

    1 - I look at my strength and resources and know I can make it work.
    5 - I look at past experience and I have confidence in the future.
    10 - I look at others and wonder how any of us are going to survive.

Subtotal F ______________

43. When I consider why I am here . . .

    1 - I have a specific calling to change people's lives.
    5 - I know I am here for a purpose and that life has meaning.
    10 - I don't know why I am here.

44. When I consider my future . . .

    1 - My future has been mapped out for me.
    5 - I am constantly getting more and more clarity about my future.
    10 - I am fearful and uncertain about what the future holds.

45. When I am faced with a choice, decision or opportunity . . .

    1 - There are no choices when on the True path.
    5 - I choose in favor of my passions.
    10 - I feel confused about which way to go.

46. When I consider who I am and how I am designed (my personality, strengths, talents) . . .

    1 - I must change myself to fulfill my mission.
    5 - I am uniquely designed to do exactly what is needed to fulfill my purpose.
    10 - I am unsure how I fit and what I am supposed to do with my life.

47. When I look at the direction my life is headed . . .

    1 - I am determinedly following the path outlined for me.
    5 - I am joyfully following a sense of purpose.
    10 - I am discouraged or depressed about the direction my life is heading.

48. When people disappoint me by making poor choices . . .

    1 - I challenge them and then avoid them in the future.
    5 - I am realistic without being cynical about their choices and seek to respond in a loving manner.
    10 - I am hurt and shut down emotionally.

49. When describing how I view the future, I would use the word . . .

    1—Realistic 5—Optimistic 10—Pessimistic

50. When I look at the impact I have . . .

    1 - I'm not sure the world is ready for my message yet.

5 - I know my life and action make a difference in the world.
10 - I don't believe I am making an impact.

Subtotal G ________________

Scoring Your Belief Quotient

I. First, add up each section for a subtotal score. Place those scores on the blanks below. Then add up each to determine your composite **Belief Quotient**.

A ______

+ B ______

+ C ______

+ D ______

+ E ______

+ F ______

+ G ______

= ________ **Composite Score**

Composite scores can be rated as follows:

301-500 Skewed Belief System

Your beliefs have been skewed and are not supporting your success optimally. You are working way too hard to achieve what you want but get in your own way over and over again. Review your sub-total scores to identify the beliefs that are sabotaging your success and work through the exercises at the end of each chapter to transform your belief system. Applying effort in the right areas will help you find success!

200-300 Optimal Belief System

Your beliefs are supporting your success most of the time. You are confident, self-assured, and emotionally healthy. For further personal growth, review your sub-total scores to see if any one area could be improved. Continue strengthening your beliefs by reading the rest of this book and working through the exercises.

1-199 Wobbly Belief System

Your beliefs have been undermined—probably by painful events in the past, low self-esteem, and a lack of clarity on your purpose in life. Use the beliefs you have that are strong to work on those that need improvement. You can have a strong healthy belief system that supports your success. Work through the chapters and exercises in this book and you will see progress.

II. Review your subtotal scores to identify strengths and weaknesses in your belief system. ***The Belief Quotient*** is based on research indicating that strengths in several key areas support a healthy belief system. The beliefs covered on this ***Belief Quotient*** assessment can be seen as a continuum, moving between skewed, strong and weak beliefs. Plot your score below to get a visual picture of your belief system:

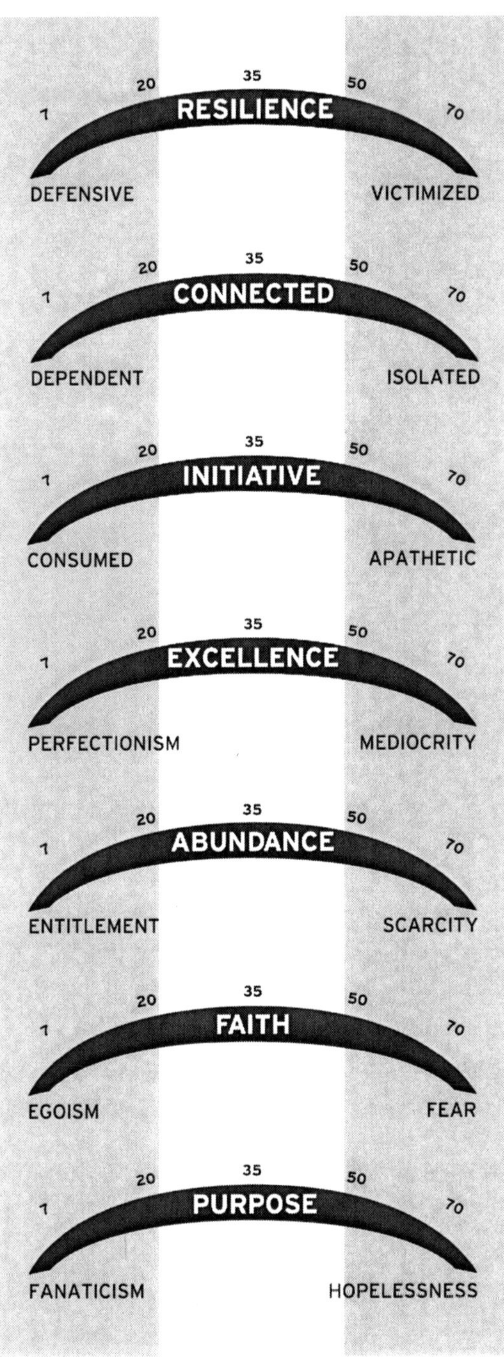

20
35
50
1
RESILIENCE
70
DEFENSIVE
VICTIMIZED
20
35
50
1
CONNECTED
70
DEPENDENT
ISOLATED
20
35
50
1
INITIATIVE
70
CONSUMED
APATHETIC
20
35
50
1
EXCELLENCE
70
PERFECTIONISM
MEDIOCRITY
20
35
50
1
ABUNDANCE
70
ENTITLEMENT
SCARCITY
20
35
50
1
FAITH
70
EGOISM
FEAR
20
35
50
1
PURPOSE
70
FANATICISM
HOPELESSNESS

EXAMPLE SCORESHEET

Name: "Cindy"

A 25

\+ B 55

\+ C 60

\+ D 65

\+ E 20

\+ F 30

\+ G 40

= 295 **Composite Score**

Note:

"Cindy's" scores place her in the Optimal Belief System range, which means she is coping fairly well with effort.

You can see that she has several areas of belief that could be strengthened. Once she shifts her negative beliefs, she will begin to find success is not nearly as hard to achieve on a consistent basis.

Cindy's individual beliefs:

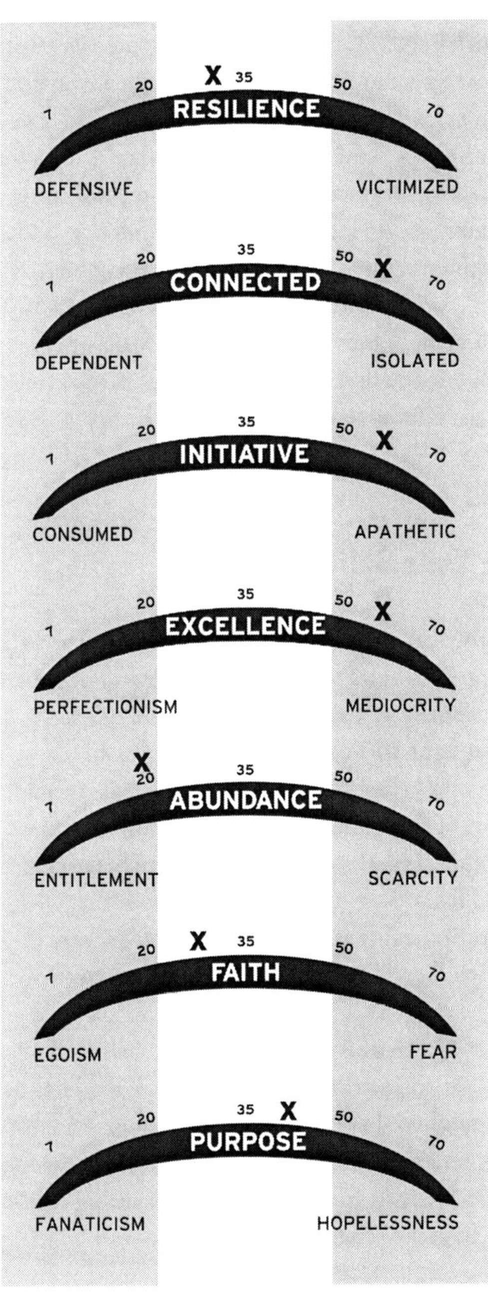

When you look at the results for Cindy's Belief Quotient Assessment, you will see that she received a composite score placing her in the Optimal Belief System range. This score fits with Cindy's life, as she appears to be doing well on the surface. Look deeper, however, and review Cindy's scores for the seven beliefs and you will discover why she is unhappy and struggling. Cindy's scores for Resilience, Faith and Purpose are in the center column, indicating that she has balance in these areas. Her score for Abundance is skewed, falling in the Entitlement range. Scores for Connectedness, Initiative and Excellence were weak. Instead of Connected, Cindy is Isolated. Instead of having Initiative, Cindy is Apathetic. Instead of Excellence, Cindy struggles with Mediocrity. Cindy's task now is to review the material on these beliefs, complete the exercises and begin to change her Belief Quotient.

Changing Your Belief Quotient

You've probably heard about how elephants are trained. A heavy chain is wrapped around a log at one end and attached to the foot of a young elephant at the other. This log is too heavy and large for the young elephant to move. But as it begins to grow, the elephant eventually becomes large and strong enough that it could move the log if it tried. Years of being unable to move the log has caused the elephant to stopped trying. The elephant has a limiting belief that it is incapable of moving the log.

What limiting belief is holding you back? Where in your life have you stopped trying? What chains are binding you to faulty ways of living?

The Belief Quotient Assessment and the Self-Reflection Questions have helped you to identify self-limiting beliefs. Now is the time to begin to change those beliefs!

There are five steps to changing a belief. Work through these steps with a specific belief in mind. As your continuing reading this book, focus on the chapter or chapters that apply to your beliefs and complete the exercises.

You can change your Belief Quotient with POWER:

P — Define the **PROBLEM** belief you want to shift?

Identify the belief that has been getting in your way and begin to think differently about it. Recognize that this belief is not immovable. Beliefs are not set in stone. Just like the elephant, you think you are permanently tethered to an immovable object, but you are not! A thought becomes a self-limiting belief because it has run through your mind that you have accepted it as truth. Your confidence in this "truth" is built on an assumed reality, not on objective truth. Now you are aware of the belief and the problems it has caused, you are poised to consciously create a new belief that supports your success.

Make sure you are attacking the root or core belief. Beliefs are like weeds. If you pull as a surface problem instead of the deeply embedded root, the belief will show up again later. Here is an example of root and surface beliefs:

Surface Belief:

"I hate making calls for my business."

This belief can create serious problems for professionals who need to make calls and set appointments in order to find and serve clients.

Core Belief

"I'm not good enough."

The surface belief ("I hate making calls") stems from an underlying belief that you are not good enough, which is connected to "I'm going to be rejected," "I can't live up to expectations," "I'm going to fail." This core belief is paralyzing and keeps you from doing what you need to do to be successful.

O — Generate **OPTIONS** beyond your existing belief? What other ways could I think and feel about this belief?

You have the power to choose your beliefs and to recognize whether certain beliefs are supportive or whether they are sabotaging you. Some beliefs are rooted in lies; others are simply the result of faulty assumptions. But every self-sabotaging belief has offered you some kind of benefit or pay off. Ask yourself: What do I get out of holding this self-limiting belief? What is the emotional pay-off that I get from this belief?

In the case of "I'm not good enough" the benefit might be that you don't have to work as hard. According to this belief, even if you were to work hard, you would never succeed. Holding the belief "I'm not good enough" gives you an excuse for apathy about your work. It's also possible that the belief "I'm not good enough" is covering a fear of failure. If you aren't good enough, you don't have to risk trying and failing. Or maybe the belief "I'm not good enough" has generated support from well-meaning people. Their pity makes you feel like they care about you and your struggle. Any of these scenarios could be emotional pay-offs for holding the belief "I'm not good enough."

Give serious thought to how you have been benefitting from your self-limiting belief.

When you recognize these options as potential alternatives to the background behind your belief, the belief is weakened.

W — **WORK** to release the belief.

Picture your limiting belief as a chair you sit on regularly. The action of sitting on that chair represents your faith that the chair will hold you up. But the chair is faulty. The legs are uneven, the back doesn't support you, and you know you need a new chair.

Imagine the seat of the chair as your core belief and each of the legs as evidence supporting that belief. Your emotions have nailed this chair to the floor and keep you from moving the chair in any direction. You're stuck.

All it takes to release the chair is to recognize that your evidence does not support your belief. Remove enough legs from the chair and it will topple over. What is the evidence you have collected to support your self-limiting belief?

If your limiting belief is "I'm not good enough", you will need to identify the evidence you have collected supporting that belief. Here are some possible legs on your chair, or the supporting evidence supporting this belief:

- "I messed up my client's paperwork."
- "I got fired from my last job."
- "I didn't get the sale."
- "I lost a client."

Take each leg and trace it back to see if it truly supports your belief that "I'm not good enough." Filling in the backstory on each piece of evidence and considering how it might NOT support your belief will cause your chair to collapse. Here's what that might look like in a chart:

Evidence	Backstory	Support my belief?
"I messed up my client's paperwork."	I didn't know I needed that new form for that policy.	NO
"I got fired from my last job."	The boss wanted to hire his son. I was the newest employee and in the way.	NO
"I didn't get the sale."	I didn't get that one, but I got 2 last week and can get more next week if I get busy.	NO

"I lost a client."	She was angry when I failed to return her call. I usually return calls within 24 hrs. but this time I messed up.	YES

In the first three rows, each piece of evidence is collapsed with the backstory. In the last row the evidence would seem to support the belief "I'm not good enough." Sometimes you do mess up . . . that doesn't mean you aren't good enough all the time. Your performance in that instance was not good enough.

Your chair might have just one or two legs, or it might have dozens. The more evidence you have collected, the more entrenched the belief has become. Objectively looking at your evidence and checking to see if the backstory supports your belief is a powerful way to cause a limiting belief to crumble.

If you've been sitting in this chair a long time, you just might get out some duct tape and try to hold it together. We want to obliterate the entire chair, not just the legs. You can do this by considering where this belief came from in the first place. For some time you have assumed this belief was true. This was a false assumption that is probably connected to an event or events in your past.

If your limiting belief is "I'm not good enough," it is possible you heard this as a child from parents, teachers or other people from your past. Who was it that told you through words or actions that you weren't good enough? You are not tracing the beginning of this belief to throw blame at anyone, but to consider options as to where this belief actually started. For example, what if a teacher told you that your writing wasn't good enough, and that you should give up your dream of being an author? Ask yourself what limiting beliefs your teacher possessed that could have caused him to say this. Is it possible that he once had a dream to publish a novel, but didn't think *he* was good enough? Self-limiting beliefs are contagious. We pass them on to one another. Who shared their self-limiting beliefs with you? Follow the chain of beliefs below:

> "I'm not good enough."
> My teacher told me I wasn't good enough.
> My teacher doesn't think *he* is good enough.
> My teacher's belief doesn't have anything to do with whether I am good enough or not.

Insert your own limiting belief and the chain of beliefs that led to it in a diagram like the one above. Looking at your belief objectively and logically will free you to take the next step: building a new belief.

E— **EVALUATE** new evidence supporting your new belief

Once you have eliminated a self-sabotaging belief, it is important to create or rebuild another in its place as quickly as possible. Choose a belief that directly challenges the old belief. If your old belief was "I'm not good enough," then you might consider replacing it with "I am worthwhile," "I am a valuable person," or even "I am an excellent salesman." Once you have selected a new belief to replace the old, self-limiting belief, it is important to find evidence to support your belief.

Your brain is works a lot like a computer. One aspect of your brain, the reticular activating system (RAS) works like a search engine in that computer. When you use a search engine like Google, you create a filter to find the phrase you type in the search bar. The search engine then finds items of relevant information among all the information available. The better you are in selecting keywords to type in the search bar, the better the results you receive. In the same way, the reticular activating system (RAS) filters out irrelevant information and captures information you have identified as important.

For example, when you are waiting for a flight at a busy airport terminal, you are confronted with lots of sensory input. There are sights, sounds, smells, tastes, and touches bombarding you all at once. It is impossible to pay attention to it all at the same time. So your

RAS filters all this information and sends your conscious mind the information you have focused on as important. If you are hungry, you will be more aware of the scents coming from the food vendors. If you are waiting to hear flight information, the flight number will stand out among all the noise coming over the PA system and catch your attention. Because your name is important to you, you will hear when it is called over the paging system whether or not you have been paying attention to the announcements. This is your RAS at work, sifting and filtering information to serve your mind.

The RAS can be a powerful ally in shifting your beliefs and achieving your goals. When you consciously choose to look for evidence to support your new beliefs, your brain will sift through all the information coming your way to find that evidence. This is an amazing feat, because it has been estimated that there are at least two million pieces of sensory information in our environment at any given time. As I write this there is a fan blowing in my office, my feet are cold, someone is watching TV somewhere in the house, my dog is snoring, and I am kind of thirsty. Until I stopped to tune into my environment and my senses, none of those things were at the front of my conscious mind. Now I have to stop and go get a drink, turn off the noisy fan, and put the dog out because I'm having trouble concentrating! My focus has shifted from this paragraph to my senses.

Your brain is only capable of handling about 134 bits of information per second. That may seem like plenty, but compared to the onslaught of data coming at you, it is miniscule. We miss a lot of information that rushes by at any given moment. But give the RAS a specific command to search for something and it will pull that piece of data out of the stream and deliver it to our consciousness.

Until now, you have not been collecting evidence for your new belief. Your brain was busy searching for information that would support your old belief. It is time to change the search command and begin to filter the data in your environment for evidence that supports your new belief. You can do this by writing down your new belief and brainstorming on the types of things that would support it. For example, if the new belief you are focusing on is "I am an excellent salesman", you will write down that belief and then suggest your RAS find evidence such as:

- I notice the body language of my potential client.
- I remember the wording of my presentation.
- I hear words of appreciate and affirmation from my clients and colleagues about my sales abilities.

When you focus your attention on these pieces of evidence, be sure to also focus your emotions. Allow yourself to imagine just what it would feel like to be an excellent salesman. How smart would you feel if suddenly you noticed the hints your potential client gave you through body language? How confident would you be if you remember the precise wording of your sales presentation? How happy would it make you to receive appreciation and affirmation about your sales abilities? Emotions raise the level of importance of a search command to the RAS. When your RAS delivers the evidence you are looking for to your conscious mind, your new belief will grow deeper and stronger.

R — **REINFORCE** your new belief

The best way to reinforce your new belief is to commit to focusing your attention on finding supportive evidence as described above. Create a daily practice when you are working with new beliefs. Commit to taking time each day to notice the evidence that has come your way. Write your experiences down and keep track of the changes you are seeing.

I also recommend you create a daily practice of repeating affirmations that support your belief. If you learn to use affirmations correctly, you will find them to be a powerful tool in reinforcing your new beliefs. At the end of Chapter 3 you will find a step by step outline for creating and using affirmations.

The rest of this book is designed to help you in further understanding your belief system and creating habits that reinforce new, supportive beliefs. Each chapter focuses on a belief continuum, describing the positive belief and the weakened or skewed beliefs associated with it. Do not feel like you have to read the chapters in order. Based on your results from the Belief Quotient assessment, choose the beliefs that concern you the most and read the chapters about those beliefs. Commit to completing the exercises at the end of each chapter. They have been designed and selected for each chapter based on the beneficial results others have received when they worked to strengthen their belief system. Determine to make building better beliefs a part of your daily routine. Your hard work will pay off. Before you know it, you will find yourself enjoying life in a whole new way with beliefs that have supported your success.

CHAPTER 3

REBUILDING RESILIENCE

[ri-**zil**-y*uh*ns] The ability to bounce back from adversity.

"Someone was hurt before you wronged before you, hungry before you, frightened before you, beaten before you, humiliated before you, raped before you . . . yet, someone survived. You can do anything you choose to do."
Maya Angelou

Chris and Mark had it rough growing up. Their mother died when they were very young and their father turned to alcohol for comfort. Their dad was a mean drunk, and he drank almost every night. The boys fended for themselves, getting to school, finding food, and staying out of their father's way as best they could. His anger was unpredictable and he beat the boys with his belt whenever he thought they were out of line. Mark, the younger of the two, had a learning disability that made reading and test taking a serious challenge at school. Chris did fairly well in school in spite of what was going on at home. Both boys graduated from high school and looked for jobs that would take them as far away from their dad as possible. Mark took a job at a small office supply store, moving boxes in the warehouse. Chris found work with a construction company and eventually apprenticed as an electrician. Things were looking up for both boys.

Chris shared a house with a few buddies who enjoyed partying on the weekends. Soon Chris was drinking heavily every weekend, and even participated in drug use and casual sex. He felt he was better than his father because he was sober during the week and was showing up for work every day. But things were not going well for Chris. Any time his boss would point out his mistakes or make suggestions on how his work could be better, Chris had a reason or excuse why he did it the way he did. When a project failed, it was someone else's fault. Chris argued, blamed, and became angry whenever he was confronted. Eventually his boss stopped trying to mentor Chris and gave the challenging projects to others who were more open. Chris felt he was being treated unfairly and that his boss "had it in for him." He began to turn to alcohol to numb his anger and bitterness.

It all came crashing down when one of Chris' one-night-stands announced that she was pregnant with his child. Chris felt that the right thing to do was to marry this woman and help her raise his child. He knew almost nothing about her. He soon learned she had two other children from other relationships, that she was unable to hold a job, and was a recovering drug user. In spite of all this, Chris kept his promise and married her. They moved into a small two-bedroom apartment and waited for the baby to be born. Chris had a lot of trouble dealing with his stepsons. Their mother was a weak disciplinarian and Chris felt they needed a firm hand. He never used his belt like his father, but he would often grab a shoulder or arm and shake it to get the child's attention. When a teacher noticed bruises on one of the boys and reported suspected child abuse to the authorities, Chris was livid. He was not a child abuser. The teacher was out of line and "had it in for him." A social worker investigated the case and recommended anger management and parenting classes for Chris. These classes interfered with his work schedule, and Chris was angry that his boss had to be told. His boss was not happy, but thought the classes might help Chris with his anger issues at work as well as at home, so he allowed Chris to leave early in order to attend the classes. Chris was on his best behavior for a while, and even slowed his drinking down while enrolled in the anger management and parenting classes. Things seemed to be getting better for Chris and his family when everything blew apart.

Chris' wife went into labor early, and due to complications, had to stay in the hospital for several days. Chris was on his own with the boys. He was stressed about the hospital bills, and frustrated with trying to get the boys to school and himself to work on time. Things at work were also stressful. Chris felt ready to explode. He drank a few beers one evening to try to take the edge off, and told the boys to get ready for bed. They had been fighting and arguing all evening and Chris had had enough. One of the boys got belligerent when Chris ordered him to bed, and Chris snapped. He grabbed the boy's arm and shook and twisted it while yelling at him. The boy screamed and cried from the pain, but Chris ignored his tears and sent him to bed. The next day Chris took the boys to the hospital to visit their mother. While they were there, Chris' wife noticed her son's bruises and how he was favoring his arm. The boy started crying and told her what had happened. A nurse overheard the story, and with his mother's permission, the boy was taken for an x-ray. The x-ray showed a fractured bone in his arm and Chris was again reported for child abuse. Chris' reaction was anger toward the nurse, his wife and his stepson. They were conspiring against him. He was not an abusive parent because he never meant to hurt anyone. Chris became so loud and threatening that the police were called and he was taken away in handcuffs.

Chris missed several days of work while in jail and while fighting the charges of child abuse in court. His boss kept his job for him, but when he returned he discovered his hours and pay had been reduced. Chris saw this as yet another example life treating him unfairly. When the courts required Chris to move out of his apartment and limit his contact with his children (including his new baby girl), he was incensed. When his wife divorced him and won custody of his child and spousal support, he again felt everyone was treating him unfairly and not listening to his side of the story.

I first heard Chris' story when his counselor called to see if I could help. Therapy was not working and both Chris and his therapist were frustrated. When Chris told me his story, I thought it had all happened recently. The pain and anger Chris felt was so raw. I was surprised to learn that Chris' baby was now a 12-year-old-girl. For over a decade, Chris has been living with the consequences of his anger and defensiveness. He has been a victim of his own making.

What was also surprising was to hear the rest of Mark's story. Chris's younger brother started out working at the office supply store warehouse, and slowly climbed the ladder, impressing his supervisors with his hard work and determination to better himself. He barely graduated from high school, but he was intelligent and resourceful. Mark was promoted from one position to the next, until his progress came to the attention of the owner. The owner spent some time with Mark and discovered they had both had painful childhoods and trouble learning in school. Mark's boss suggested that he might be dyslexic and thought he should get some testing. When his learning disability was confirmed, Mark realized that he qualified for academic support at the local college and signed up for classes. It took him nearly eight years of night classes, but Mark eventually graduated with his degree in business. His company helped pay for the classes and even gave him a promotion when he graduated. Mark was now director of operations in his company, happily married, and has two children. Mark was not a victim of his childhood or of bad choices.

Bouncing Back

What made the difference between these two young men? They were raised in the same family and endured the same poverty, humiliation and abuse. Mark probably had an even tougher time with school being another source of humiliation and defeat. Some would say that Chris' use of drugs and alcohol were the cause of his problems, but addictions are a symptom, not a root cause. The primary difference between these two young men is their beliefs about their own resilience.

Resilience is the ability to bounce back from adversity, to come through tough times and be stronger, richer, wiser and much better for the experience.[1] Resilience is based on the belief that you have value. It is the belief that even if you are knocked down over and over, you can and will get up again and again and again. Believing you are resilient creates a determination to survive and overcome overwhelming odds.

"People who soar are those who refuse to sit back, sigh and wish things would change. They neither complain of their lot nor passively dream of some distant ship coming in. Rather, they visualize in their minds that they are not quitters; they will not allow life's circumstances to push them down and hold them under." Charles Swindoll

The Erosion of Resilience

Highway 1 is known for breathtaking views of the California coastline. Over the years wind and water have pounded and eaten away at that coastline, particularly an area known as the Devil's Slide. The hillside has eroded into jagged cliffs, making the road impassable. Like Highway 1, resilience is not destroyed overnight. Resilience is eroded over time with one emotional insult after another eating away at your sense of worth.

If your resilience has been eroded, it is likely you have thoughts like these running through your mind:

- I'm not (smart, good, attractive, wealthy, educated, whatever) enough.
- I'm too damaged.
- It's too late for me.
- I'll just get hurt again.
- I brought this mistreatment on myself.

There are many reasons why you hold these self-sabotaging beliefs. John Marquez, author of *The Ultimate Journey*, has identified "6 H's" that can erode our resilience if we fail to deal with them:

1. Hurts: painful things that happened in the past
2. Horrors: scary things that happen and the fear that follows
3. Humiliations: embarrassing and shaming experiences

4. Hatreds: unresolved anger and bitterness experienced through abuse and rejection
5. Hungers: unmet needs from neglect
6. Honors: accomplishments that make you feel you have to continue to perform well to be loved and respected[2]

For most of us, resilience is undermined in early childhood. We hear messages that we aren't good enough, that our dreams are foolish, and that we can't possibly succeed. We're given degrading nicknames and are teased and bullied on the playground. Teachers tell us what is wrong with our work and not what is right with it. Our bodies are compared to glossy images on screen and in magazines, and we can never live up to their air-brushed perfection. All of this happens in what is considered a "normal" up-bringing. Add the pain of divorce, addictions, or mental health issues to a family, and a child's chance of growing up with a strong sense of self is very limited.

And yet, some do survive. Some kids grow and develop a drive and determination to succeed. Even if your self-esteem was bashed and your belief in resilience was crushed, you can recreate it. In fact, you must. Resilience is a foundational belief critical to the development and support of other beliefs required for success. The first step is to recognize your need to let go of any victim mentality or defensiveness you have developed in the place of resilience.

It is possible that your experience is very different from Chris' story. You might have been raised in a healthy home, but were victimized later by what Marquez calls "horrors." Resilience is eroded when memories of a traumatic event are relived in the mind over and over again. Your ability to respond with resilience after a traumatic event is influenced by a number of factors including:

- Your stress level—If you are already loaded with stress over health, financial or relationship issues, you will have a harder time recovering from trauma.
- Your gender—Females tend to be more empathetic and sensitive, and tend to internalize anxiety. Males tend to be more action oriented and tend to externalize their anxiety.

The more you internalize stress, the more difficult it will be to recover from trauma.

- Your age—Middle aged individuals tend to carry more stress and responsibilities for their children and parents, and therefore react more strongly to traumatic events.
- Your brain—Research indicates that individuals with a smaller than average hippocampus are predisposed toward developing Post-Traumatic Stress Disorder. The hippocampus is an area of the brain responsible for storage and retrieval of memories and emotions. Studies show that a smaller hippocampus decrease resilience. In addition, on-going stress can generate hormones like cortisol which shrink the hippocampus, creating even less ability to rebound after traumatic events.[3]

Horrors and humiliations can happen at home, work or school: any place where you should have a reasonable sense of safety, but that safety is destroyed by coldness and cruelty. One in three women is the victim of some kind of domestic violence or assault. Spousal abuse, committed by either the wife or the husband, can destroy a sense of self-worth and undermine resilience. Humiliations can be linked to hurts or horrors or be separate experiences. In Chris' story he describes the humiliation of being taken away to jail in handcuffs in front of his stepsons as one of the worst things to ever happen to him. The shame he felt that day was just as painful as what he experienced when he was beaten by his drunken father. His hatred of his father's abuse was something that lived within Chris on an unconscious level and shaped his responses to authority figures throughout his life. Although, he was hungry for love and affection, he numbed those yearnings with casual sex and substance abuse.

Chris also struggled with something psychologists call "learned helplessness." Learned helplessness is a condition that grows out of the depression resulting from defeat and abuse.[4] Whenever Chris achieved any measure of success at school or work, he would unknowingly begin to sabotage himself. The idea of trying to live up to any expectation of success was too much for Chris. When he did well on a test, it had to be a fluke. He knew he would fail miserably on the next one—and he did. When his boss complimented him on mastering a new task at work,

Chris would struggle for weeks to rise to that level of mastery again. Learned helplessness causes us to miss opportunities, to fail to act when escape is possible, and to keep us trapped in patterns of failure.

Victim Mentality and Defensiveness

When someone has been beaten down emotionally over and over, a victim mentality develops. More blows are expected to come. A victim mentality is characterized by a sense of powerlessness over life's circumstances. Feeling victimized is different than a victim mentality. You feel victimized when you have been harmed. You have a victim mentality when you expect to be harmed again. Feeling victimized stems from a healthy sense of justice and preservation. Survivors feel victimized, but are able to see themselves as overcoming their oppressors.[5] Having a victim mentality is taking on the role of the victim in life and feeling that life is happening outside of you. You passively watch as the life you want slips away and you feel unable to take action to change your circumstances. Psychologically, a victim mentality is very destructive. Depression and hopelessness become constant companions. A pervasive sense of helplessness can lead to pessimism, negative thinking, and strong feelings of guilt and shame.

Owners of a victim mentality usually fail to accept responsibility for their choices and actions. When a victim fails to recover their resilience, they become defensive. The slightest suggestion that a mistake has been made or that a wrong has been done feels like an attack.

Definition of defensiveness

Your unconscious mind develops defense mechanisms as a way to protect yourself from harm. Psychologists have identified 15 common defense mechanisms, listed here from the most primitive to the most mature:

Immature Defense Mechanisms

1. Denial: refusing to accept reality or fact
2. Regression: reverting to an earlier stage of development
3. Acting Out: engaging in extreme behavior to express thoughts or feelings
4. Dissociation: losing track of time and/or person, and finding another representation of the self in order to continue in the moment
5. Compartmentalization: separating parts of oneself from awareness of other parts and behaving as if one had separate sets of values
6. Projection: attributing undesired thoughts, feelings or impulses onto another person who does not have those thoughts, feelings or impulses
7. Reaction formation: converting unwanted or dangerous thoughts, feelings or impulses into their opposites (e.g., acting excessively kind when feeling angry)

Less Immature Defense Mechanisms

8. Repression: unconscious blocking of unacceptable thoughts, feelings and impulses
9. Displacement: redirecting of thoughts feelings and impulses directed at one person or object and taking them out upon another person or object
10. Intellectualization: overemphasizing thinking when confronted with an unacceptable impulse, situation or behavior
11. Rationalization: putting something into a different light or offering a different explanation for one's perceptions or behaviors in the face of a changing reality (e.g., making excuses)
12. Undoing: attempting to take back an unconscious behavior or thought that is unacceptable or hurtful

Mature Defense Mechanisms

13. Sublimation: channeling of unacceptable impulses, thoughts and emotions into more acceptable ones
14. Compensation: counterbalancing perceived weaknesses by emphasizing strength in other arenas
15. Assertiveness: emphasizing one's needs or thoughts in a manner that is respectful, direct and firm[6]

Identifying primitive defense mechanisms is an important step toward changing defensive behavior and rebuilding true resilience. Like so many of our behaviors, defense mechanisms can be passed on from one generation to another. Methods of coping with stress and threatening situations become unconscious patterns in our lives. Members of families, businesses, and other organizations can develop defensive patterns of interacting and reacting to one another. It is not always easy to own up to immature or primitive behavior, but once you recognize your defense mechanisms you will be ready to rebuild resilience and a healthier, more successful way of handling challenges.

Resilience and Your Belief Quotient

Your Belief Quotient score indicates where you fall on the Resilience continuum. If you rated yourself as being fairly adaptable and able to bounce back from hardship, your score landed in the center of the arc on Resilience. But if you described yourself as still struggling with wounds from the past, lacking direction and fearing failure, your scores probably landed to the right side of the arc, indicating that you see yourself as a **victim**. If the choices you made on the assessment landed on the left side of the arc, you tend to feel **defensive**. VICTIMIZED is the damaged or weakened belief. DEFENSIVE is the skewed belief. Often individuals will try to regain resilience by overcompensating and becoming defensive. **Defensiveness is resistance to what is.** Instead of resolving the past and reclaiming the future, defensiveness fights with the past and stumbles through the future. It is only by finding balance and rebuilding resilience that we can find success in life.

> *"When you become defensive, blame others, and do not accept and surrender to the moment, your life meets resistance. Any time you encounter resistance, recognize that if you force the situation, the resistance will only increase. You don't want to stand rigid like a tall oak that cracks and collapses in the storm. Instead, you want to be flexible, like a reed that bends with the storm and survives."*
>
> *Deepak Choprah*

It was hard to see an intelligent man like Chris throw away his gifts and talents. His life was stalled in a vicious circle of defeat as he went back and forth from a victim mentality to immature defensiveness. Accepting responsibility for his actions was the hardest thing for him to do. Recognizing the defensive patterns of behavior and developing more mature ways to cope with life's challenges takes a great deal of perseverance. Chris has a long way to go, but he is rebuilding resilience.

> *"Surviving is coping. Thriving is creating."*
>
> *Dr. Paul Pearsall*

Marcy's Story

Marcy is a divorced mother of four who works from home. After years of working in healthcare, she created a home-based business in order to spend more time with her children and see that they got to all their sporting events, concerts, rehearsals, and other activities. Marcy wants her kids to experience childhood differently than she did. Her upbringing was strict, cold, and critical. Nothing was ever good enough for Marcy's father and he criticized her relentlessly. Her mother watched Marcy being beaten down emotionally over and over, but never intervened because she did not feel it was her place as a wife. Marcy also had an older brother who was allowed to bully and at times beat her. It is not surprising that Marcy married early to get away from home. Her husband was charming and kind early in their relationship, but once they were married he became more and more controlling. He was self-centered and sarcastic, and felt he owed Marcy no explanation for his actions or behavior. Their marriage ended when he grew tired of his responsibilities, and Marcy was left to support and raise her children alone.

As a single adult on her own, Marcy had the opportunity to create a new life free from the pain of the past. But Marcy was locked into patterns of victimization and defensiveness. When I first began to work with Marcy on expanding her business, I noticed a lack of resilience when times were tough. Businesses are run by people, and when they are not working well, it is often because of actions taken based on faulty belief systems. Marcy's business was suffering because of a lack of healthy boundaries with her customers. Marcy would allow customers to walk all over her, take advantage, and criticize her award-winning work in order to avoid payment. Marcy was failing to establish limits and clear policies and procedures in her business because she had never learned to create healthy boundaries in her personal life. Marcy was still allowing her father and ex-husband to come into her home and criticize her and beat her down emotionally in front of her children. She didn't know how to stop them without getting angry, so she withdrew and pretended everything was fine. She was in denial about their abuse, compartmentalizing her emotions and reacting to their mistreatment of her with a false sweetness that felt toxic. Worse yet, her older children were beginning to act just like their grandfather and father. Her oldest son was avoiding responsibility and ignoring his mother's rules and her teenage daughter was openly critical and unkind. Marcy felt like a failure as a mother—the one thing most important to her.

Marcy was suffering from a damaged belief system. Her belief in her own resilience had been eroded and she was bouncing back and forth between victimization and defensiveness. Her lack of resilience was affecting her business, her children, her health, her faith, and her relationships. When resilience is eroded, your beliefs around connections with others, initiative, excellence, abundance, faith and purpose also come under attack. This was true for Marcy and you will see how raising her Belief Quotient in each of these areas is transforming her life.

Rebuilding Resilience

Victimization and defensiveness are reactive. Resilience is proactive. To rebuild resilience you must make a conscious choice to face the anger, fear and pain of the past. **Taking personal control and responsibility for your reactions and behavior is necessary to rebuild resilience.** You must develop a willingness to create meaningful connections with others, which requires you to be open, curious and discerning. By becoming more objective about yourself, seeing yourself accurately and treating yourself with compassion you will be prepared to adapt to changes and challenges in your life.

We teach others how we want to be treated. Until we can treat ourselves with compassion, we cannot expect others to treat us with kindness and respect. Self-compassion involves generating feelings of kindness and care toward ourselves. This type of compassion can reduce anxiety, making us more resilient in the face of challenges. When we care for ourselves, we are motivated to make positive changes based on our heart's desires rather than criticism or negative influences. Self-compassion is a stepping stone to self-esteem and confidence.

Self-compassion can easily be confused with self-pity. If you find yourself rehearsing your wounds from the past (aloud or internally) you could be re-wounding yourself and sinking deeper into despair. life coach Martha Beck suggests three reasons why you might want to talk about negative experiences:

- When you are lost in your darkness and revealing your story will lead you to people of compassion
- When talking about your struggle can help others with the same problem
- When talking shines a spotlight on injustice or cruelty that flourishes in the dark created by secrets

Self-pity is the fine line between heroic storytelling from psychological rumination. Self-pity extorts attention. When shedding light by telling your story, you feel wrenching pain, grief, anger, or shame. Someone looking for sympathy will feel less pain, even numb. Obsessing aloud is fishing for pity. Grieving will bring comfort from others, where demanding pity will repel them.

Compulsively examining a story increases your sorrow and can become a habit. When you catch yourself ruminating on the past in an unhealthy way, use Beck's phrase to stop rehearsing:

Am I presently learning the truth about my life's work?

1. Be present

Create an anchor by establishing a simple, physical, factual connection with present reality. This will loosen the grip of the past and bring you into the present.

2. Never stop learning

Take your old story and treat it like a hypothesis that must be proven. Ex: "I'm not good enough." Is easily disproven when any objective evidence shows up that someone, even your dog, thinks you are good enough for them.

3. Insist on the truth

You can change a belief about yourself and your past when you insist on the truth you've learned. Hanging on to partial truths and embellishments from our past is often an excuse we create to avoid facing or doing the hard things in our present.

4. Put all your energy into your life's work

Freedom from the past and from self-pity opens doors to identifying your life's work. One small step toward your purpose will pull you from the quicksand of the past.[7]

Scientists studying post-traumatic stress disorder have noticed that certain people rebound from their experience stronger as a result of the challenges they faced.[8] This growth is due to four types of resilience that can be developed by making small changes day by day.

1. Physical resilience: Every moment that you spend moving builds physical resilience, adding years to your life and confidence in your outlook. Studies show that simply getting up out of your chair and taking a few steps can make a difference in the brain's perception of emotional and physical pain.
2. Mental resilience: Will power grows stronger with exercise. A person who has been traumatized physically or emotionally can become so defeated that they lose the will to live. This can also be true of those who have been suffering from a chronic illness. You can strengthen your mental will power with puzzles, games, and simple counting exercises.
3. Emotional resilience: In Chapter 1 you learned about Dr. Barbara Frederickson's research on replacing negative emotions with positive emotions. In her book *Positivity,* Dr. Frederickson says that we need a ratio of three positive emotions for every negative emotion to create a positive emotional outlook. These positive emotions can be generated by activities as simple as looking at something beautiful, by smiling at someone you

love, or experiencing curiosity about what is outside your window.

4. Social resilience: You can increase your social resilience through touch and gratitude. When you reach out and touch someone for several seconds with a simple handshake, your brain receives a boost in oxytocin, known as the trust hormone.[9] If your resilience has been wounded, immature defense mechanisms may hold you back from the comforting touch of a trusted friend or loved one. The very act of touching someone for a few seconds will create the brain chemistry needed to recreate trust. Gratitude is also challenging for someone who has been injured by others, but rebuilding a habit of expressing appreciation with recreate the social connections needed to reclaim resilience.

Jane McGonigal is a game designer. After a concussion failed to heal properly she suffered from excruciating headaches, brain fog, and mental confusion. It seemed as though the pain would never stop, and she began to think about ending her life. Instead of allowing herself to become a victim of her injury, Jane began to research how she could heal her brain. She came upon the research I've quoted above and decided to create a tool that would help her rebuild resilience physically, mentally, emotionally and socially. Jane used her talents as a game developer to create SuperBetter, an online game that helped her become the hero battling the enemy depression and pain. Jane recovered from her injury and shared her experience at a TED conference, making the point that through simple activities we can rebuild resilience and live longer, happier lives.[10]

You are stronger than you know.
You are surrounded by potential allies.
You will soon conquer a challenge.
You are a hero to others. You are getting SuperBetter.

Affirmations

One way to increase self-compassion and resilience is to create "I am" statements or affirmations. Affirmations have been mocked and misunderstood by many. Please do not overlook the power of a positive affirmation to shift your thoughts and beliefs.[11] Here is how you can create powerful, belief-shifting affirmations:

1. Start your affirmation with the words "I am". "I AM" is a name for God, and you are claiming Divine power and intervention when you start your affirmation this way. You can also start affirmations with words like "I know", "I have", and "I love".
2. Write your affirmation in the positive. If you focus on a statement like "I am not angry with my abuser anymore", your focus is on the negative (in this case the abuser). Instead write a statement like "I have forgiven those who have harmed me and I am free from the wounds of the past."
3. Write your affirmation in present tense. Even if you are not yet experiencing your affirmation, write and visualize it as if it were happening in this moment. This will shift your unconscious mind into making the statement true.
4. Use your own words and language that is comfortable for you. You want to use words that feel right on the tongue when you say them out loud.
5. Write your affirmations with passion and feeling. Your "I am" statements should be charged with warmth and make you feel energized, happy, and peaceful. Your affirmations will carry more power if your mind and emotions are engaged.
6. Engage your senses as you write and repeat your affirmations. Use rich, colorful language that creates pictures of the life you want. Write your affirmations on special paper with appealing fonts or script. Listen to music as you read and repeat your affirmations. If you enjoy incense, potpourris, or other room scents, use them.
7. Focus on the "what", not the "how". Let your mind examine what you want to be true, but do not let it question how it will

happen. Your mind will limit the endlessly perfect possibility of how your future will unfold.

8. Incorporate your current successes and positive traits. As you focus on the life you want to create, recognize what you already love about yourself and your life. For example, "I am building my life upon truth because I have faced my fears and am strong and resilient.
9. Write affirmations about your deepest desires. Ask yourself:

    - What thinking patterns or beliefs would I like to change?
    - What circumstances would I like to improve or transform?
    - What experiences would I like to have?
    - What feelings would I like to enjoy?
    - What do I want my life to be like?

10. Write incremental affirmations. In addition to writing powerful statements of where you want to be, write affirmations that capture the truth of where you are now. If your limiting belief has been, "I'm not good enough," the affirmation "I am good enough" or "I am worthy" might be too big of a leap for you. Create an affirmation that bridges the gap like "I am kind and caring toward others." This affirmation reinforces your worth and prepares you for more.

You can write as many or as few affirmations as you like. You might make a list of several and rotate through them over the course of a week or month. Take time to read through each of your affirmations, letting the words and ideas sink in before moving on to the next.

"I am" statements for resilience:

- I am safe and secure.
- I am free of the past—it has no power over me.
- I am forgiving myself and those around me.

- I am (smart, good, attractive, wealthy, educated, whatever) enough for anything I need to do or be.
- I am beautiful, intelligent, and designed with purpose.
- I am healthy and whole.
- I am confident and looking forward to all that life will bring.

The exercises at the end of this chapter are designed to help you strengthen your sense of self. The quality of your life will improve immeasurably when you commit to increasing resilience.

EXERCISES to Rebuild Resilience

1. Awareness Exercise

Going through life with a victim mentality actually has some benefits or you wouldn't do it. One of the first steps toward eliminating a victim mentality is to identify how you have been benefiting from this attitude. Take out a piece of paper and write a few lines on what you have gotten out of a victim mentality. Here are a few suggestions:

- You get attention and support from others when you are a victim. At least until they grow weary of being the hero and want a more balanced relationship.
- You don't have to stretch and grow when you are a victim. Being a victim means being safe. You don't have to take risks and fear failure or rejection.
- You don't have anyone depending on you.
- You don't have to take responsibility for your life and your mistakes. Someone else will bail you out if you are pitiful enough.
- You ____
- You ____

2. Dig for the Truth

If you feel you've been repressing the truth of past wounds, work through these exercises in your journal:

- What do I almost know?
- What do I almost feel?
- What would I want to do if it weren't forbidden?
- What am I tired of hiding from myself?
- What subjects do I not let myself think about?
- What is it that my family and I all know but no one ever talks about?

3. Radical Responsibility

Resilience requires that we take responsibility for our lives. When we accept responsibility for our own success, our confidence and sense of self grows.[12] Instead of waiting for validation or support from others, begin to find the courage to practice radical responsibility. Every time you are faced with a challenge, a failure, or a frustration ask how you have contributed to the problem. Did you bounce a check? Take responsibility for your finances and commit to being more organized and disciplined. Is someone angry with you? Take responsibility for how you might have offended them. Are you stuck in a job you hate? Take responsibility for your future and take steps to move forward. You are not blaming yourself, but are being proactive in seeing how your actions and attitudes have created your current reality.

Today I'm taking responsibility for ____________________________.
I am committing to take the following action:
____.

4. Find the Blessings

Behind every painful trial or challenge in our lives there are blessings. Identifying how a hardship has benefitted you will take you from *victim* to *victor.*

List 3 painful or challenging experiences:

1. ____
2. ____
3. ____

Now look back and find the blessings for each of these experiences. How did you grow? What did you learn?

Challenge 1 Blessings:

1. ______________________________
2. ______________________________
3. ______________________________

Challenge 2 Blessings:

1. ______________________________
2. ______________________________
3. ______________________________

Challenge 3 Blessings:

1. ______________________________
2. ______________________________
3. ______________________________

Meditate on these blessings and continue to look for more!

5. Do The Work

The Work by Byron Katie is a way of identifying and questioning the thoughts that cause all the fear, violence, depression, frustration, and suffering you experience.[13] *The Work* can be found at http://www.thework.com with videos and worksheets you can download at no charge. You can do *The Work* on your own, but I highly recommend working with a trained facilitator.

6. Create a Gratitude Practice

This topic will be covered in more depth in Chapter 7, but begin to create a gratitude practice as you reflect on resilience. When we struggle with a victim mentality and defensiveness, we fail to look beyond our own pain. Instead of asking "Why me?", ask "why not me?". Your gratitude practice at this point might start with focusing on how things could be worse, but over time it will develop into genuine thankfulness for the gifts you have been given. To complete this exercise, list 10 things you are grateful for every day for a week and see how your attitude changes!

7. Let It Go

Forgiveness is a tricky subject to address when you are struggling with eroded resilience. Forgiveness is NOT ignoring a wrong or overlooking how someone has injured you. Forgiveness is untying your emotional knots and finding freedom from the bondage. You are releasing any sense that someone owes you anything like an apology or restitution. When you forgive, you will let go of the resentment that poisoned your chance to rebuild resilience.

I am releasing ______________________________ from my anger and resentment and no longer expect anything from him/her/them.

8. Install a Sentry

Imagine a Gatekeeper at the entryway to your mind stopping and examining every thought that attempts to come through. Your Gatekeeper stops the negative thoughts from entering or loitering around your mind. Thoughts like "You can't do that: you'll never succeed" are banished and replaced with "I can do this as well or better than anyone else." What thoughts need banished or replaced in your thinking? Put a sentry or gatekeeper to work by observing your thoughts and deciding consciously whether they are thoughts you want taking residence in your mind.

9. Consult an Expert

You are most likely familiar with the acronym WWJD for What Would Jesus Do. When you are faced with a challenging situation that makes you feel insecure, you can consult an expert in your mind to find support and creative solutions. My panel of experts includes Jesus, the Dalai Lama, Madame Curie, Jack Canfield, Napoleon Hill, and my Grandpa Charlie Van Allen. When I am faced with an intimidating home repair, I ask myself "What would Grandpa Charlie do?" and I am always surprised at how easy the task becomes. When I need to resolve a conflict with someone, I consult with Jesus and the Dalai Lama and come away with fresh insight and a peaceful solution. The amazing thing about consulting an expert in your mind is that you are actually asking yourself for answers, but finding support and unique ways of doing things when you consider how an iconic figure would solve your problem. Create your panel of experts here.

My panel of experts includes:

____

____

____

____

____

10. Rehearsal

The neural pathways created in your brain when you pretend, rehearse or visualize are the same pathways used when you actually do something. "See" yourself achieving your goal and you will be actually making it happen.

11. What If?

Victims often live in the land of "what if". "What if everything goes wrong?" "What if they reject me?" or "What if I look like an idiot?"

Turn your "what if" into a positive. Instead of "What if everything goes wrong?" ask "What if everything goes right?" Rather than "What if they reject me?" ask "What if they love me?" Forcing yourself to consider a positive outcome will shift you from a victim mentality to an empowered outlook.

11. Watch Your Language!

Become aware of how your language is affecting your mood and your outcomes. Words are powerful—choose them carefully.[14] Certain words and phrases can create the opposite effect you want. Use wording with a positive focus rather than a negative one. When you say, "Don't trip on that rug," you are actually reinforcing the idea of tripping on the rug. Instead try saying "Watch your step". The exception to this is when the object of the sentence is the outcome you want. "I don't feel well" puts focus on feeling well and is better than saying "I am sick". Make sure your words say exactly what you mean to say. To implement this, find someone to hold you accountable for what comes out of your mouth. Ask them to stop you and have you reword things in the positive.

12. Take Small Steps

Take small steps every day to strengthen all four types of resilience: physical, mental, emotional and social. You can create your own exercises, or visit www.SuperBetter.com and enjoy playing a game designed to rebuild resilience.

What other exercises help you rebuild and strengthen your resilience? Share your ideas online at http://www.beliefquotient.com

CHAPTER 4

CREATING CONNECTEDNESS

[ka-nek'-ted-nes] Joined or linked together;
state of being in relationship.

*"'I' cannot reach fulfillment without 'thou.'
The self cannot be self without other selves. Self-concern
without other-concern is like a tributary that has no
outward flow to the ocean."
Martin Luther King, Jr.*

*"It is not good for man to be alone."
Genesis 2:1*

We are designed for relationship. A person's ability to connect and create healthy interpersonal relationships is critical to growth, satisfaction and success. Creating and maintaining connections has a major impact on brain development in childhood and on our mental and physical health as we grow to adulthood. Relationships have a beginning, a life of their own, and an ending. They tend to grow and improve gradually, as people get to know each other and become closer emotionally; or they gradually deteriorate as people drift apart, move on with their lives and form new relationships. Healthy relationships have boundaries that are respected and maintained. In a supportive environment you are vulnerable, open to new ideas, and able to build trust. What you believe about your ability to connect with others affects every area of your life.

Your beliefs about your relationships with others are powerful predictors of your happiness and your success. **Connectedness is that ability to create and sustain meaningful, mutually beneficial relationships with others and yourself.** When you believe you are able to maintain these healthy relationships, life is balanced with support, encouragement and accountability. Without balanced relationships you risk falling into isolation or dependence.

> *"The Fijians are aware of a basic human law. We are a part of each other's reality. There is no such thing as passing someone and not acknowledging your moment of connection, not letting others know their effect on you and seeing yours on them."*
>
> *Rachel Remen, MD*

Isolation and Dependence

Dr. Brené Brown is a research professor at the University of Houston where she has spent the past decade studying vulnerability, courage, worthiness, and shame. She gained national recognition when her talk on the power of vulnerability became one of the most watched videos on TED.com with over 5 million viewers.[1] Dr. Brown touched a raw nerve desperate for comfort. We all recognize that hunger in ourselves, because connection is essential to our existence. As Dr. Brown interviewed people she discovered that connection requires excruciating vulnerability. "When asked about love, people tell you about heartbreak. When asked about connection, they tell you about loneliness."[2] Those with a sense of worthiness have a strong sense of love and belonging. They believe they are worthy of connection.

It is rare, if not impossible, to find someone who has not been wounded by the people who should be invested in supporting and encouraging them. Our parents, siblings, friends, lovers, co-workers all have one thing in common: they are human and because of that they will fail us. The negative beliefs and emotions that are born from these wounds create a sense of worthlessness and shame. Once resilience has been damaged, beliefs around your ability to create healthy relationships are affected. Isolation and dependence are at opposite ends of the connectedness continuum. Isolation can be the result of the defense mechanisms described in the last chapter. A false sense of self-preservation drives us to put up walls to prevent new hurts before they happen. There is an injustice to this defensive posture as we hold ourselves from new connections because of what someone else did to us. The problem with this is that we are assuming this new connection will be just as harmful as the ones that hurt. We fail to realize this new connection could bring healing and joy to our lives.

Social relationships have significant effects on physical and mental health. Captors use isolation to torture prisoners of war with drastic results: mental and physical breakdown and even death.[3] Isolation is imposed on us when a loved one dies or a relationship ends. Grief and depression are common. In the case of prisoners of war or the suddenly single, these individuals did not want to be alone. Self-imposed isolation, however, can be even more destructive. I am not referring to the choice to pull away for a time to reflect and refresh, but to the tendency to avoid connections with others because of fear-based thinking.

The *Diagnostic and Statistical Manual of Mental Disorders (DSMIV-TR)* describes an avoidant personality as "characterized by a pervasive pattern of social inhibition, feelings of inadequacy, extreme sensitivity to negative evaluation, and avoidance of social interaction."[4] Only 1% of the population meets the criteria for this diagnosis, because someone with avoidant personality disorder does not believe their fears are excessive and are convinced that they are inadequate, unlovable, broken, etc. But how many of us have some degree of the qualities associated with this destructive condition? The World Health Organization ICD-10 lists the following traits of an avoidant personality:

1. Persistent and pervasive feelings of tension and apprehension;
2. Belief that one is socially inept, personally unappealing, or inferior to others;
3. Excessive preoccupation with being criticized or rejected in social situations;
4. Unwillingness to become involved with people unless certain of being liked;
5. Restrictions in lifestyle because of need to have physical security;
6. Avoidance of social or occupational activities that involve significant interpersonal contact because of fear of criticism, disapproval, or rejection. Associated features may include hypersensitivity to rejection and criticism.[5]

How many of these traits describe you and how you feel about your ability to connect with others? These traits are usually developed in childhood where neglect, bullying or abuse eroded any belief that you have value and something worthwhile to contribute to others. Each negative trait interferes with your ability to create meaningful relationships. You may not have a full blown personality disorder, but your beliefs hinder your potential for success and satisfaction. At the core of this isolation is anxiety and fear. You believe you will be rejected, disliked, mistreated, so you retreat to the safety of your own company. But even there you find no peace, because you continue to berate yourself for your inability to connect.

At the other end of the spectrum from isolation is dependence. Dependence is relying on or requiring the help of something or someone, and it can become a compulsive or chronic need. You can be as addicted to a relationship as you can to drugs or alcohol. When we feel inadequate within ourselves to handle life's challenges, we turn to others for support. This is a healthy, natural response unless that relationship fails to help us grow stronger and more resilient. Dependence is a failure to take responsibility for our own emotional needs. We latch on to others and expect them to fill the holes in our emotional bucket. Emotional responsibility means recognizing that we create our own feelings and that what we feel does not come from others or circumstances. No one can make you feel angry or hurt or rejected. The feeling comes from a reaction within you. An emotionally healthy person recognizes their own worth and value and does not base it on what others say or do.

Codependence takes dependence even further and attempts to control or manipulate others. Codependency describes behaviors, thoughts and feelings that go beyond normal kinds of self-sacrifice or caretaking. It usually occurs in relationships where one is addicted to a destructive substance or behavior and the other is addicted to rescuing or fixing that person.[6] Neither dependence nor co-dependence is based on love. They are both self-centered and destructive. The belief that you need someone else to survive undermines your worth, values, and expectations from life. True connectedness is mutually beneficial, based in love, not fear.

> *"Owning our story can be hard but not nearly as difficult as spending our lives running from it. Embracing our vulnerabilities is risky but not nearly as dangerous as giving up on love and belonging and joy—the experiences that make us the most vulnerable. Only when we are brave enough to explore the darkness will we discover the infinite power of our light."*
>
> *Brené Brown*

Greg & Sheri's Story

A woman named Sheri complained that her fiancé Greg was holding back emotionally. A conversation with the two of them revealed Greg had been hurt in previous relationships. Years ago a former girlfriend had cheated on him, and less than a year ago his former wife had died of cancer. I asked a few questions about Greg's childhood friendships and learned that up until fourth grade, Greg had a large circle of friends. At that point, Greg's family moved to a new neighborhood, and Greg had a hard time finding friends. One boy in his class picked on him constantly and humiliated him to the point where Greg felt ostracized and isolated. A pattern of isolation developed, and Greg kept to himself through the rest of his school years. He had adequate grades and excelled at sports, and these two things helped him survive what could have been a very painful childhood.

After hearing Greg's story, I told the couple that I thought they should think about putting their plans on hold. They were not ready to get married. Both Sheri and Greg had emotional issues that would keep their relationship from growing. Greg was dealing with abandonment issues and grief from his former girlfriend and his wife. Both women had left him, even if his wife had no choice in the matter. He also had a long-term habit of keeping his thoughts and feelings to himself. He was holding back emotionally and treating Sheri as if she could not be trusted, like the other women in his life who had disappointed him. Greg knew he had a problem, but he didn't know what to do about it.

Sheri was equally unprepared to get married because she was settling: she needed higher expectations of her prospective partner. Her willingness to accept an engagement from an emotionally remote man indicated her lack of belief that she deserved love, support and commitment from her partner. Sheri was oblivious that her tendency toward dependence pushed Greg even further into his protective shell. Even though they loved each other, their relationship was doomed under these conditions. Sheri and Greg agreed to hold off on setting a date for their wedding and began working on their issues. You can find several of the exercises Sheri and Greg used at the end of this chapter. After a few months of dedicated work, Sheri and Greg were ready to plan their wedding. They are now happily married and raising their young son. They make time every day to check in with one another and connect.

Developing Connectedness

Psychologist George Levinger has described five stages of development for a healthy relationship:

1. **Becoming acquainted.** Getting to know and trust another person is dependent on your previous relationships. It is also

affected by first impressions, frequency of contact, and other factors. If two people find they like one another, they can move on to the next stage, but the acquaintance phase can go on indefinitely.

2. **Building**. During this stage, people begin to trust and care about each other. During this phase you look at compatibility based on background, values, goals, etc.
3. **Deepening**. A mutual commitment to a long-term friendship, romantic relationship, or other commitment is required for a relationship to deepen. This state requires time, mutual trust and commitment.
4. **Deteriorating**. Not all relationships deteriorate, but those that do tend to have common problem areas. Poor communication and a failure to share openly will create boredom, resentment, and dissatisfaction. Loss of trust and betrayals may take place as the downward spiral continues, eventually ending the relationship. If the parties find a way to resolve their problems and reestablish trust, they will go back to the building phase.
5. **Terminating**. The final stage marks the end of the relationship. Relationships end by death in the case of a healthy relationship, by mutual agreement, or by forced separation.

Levinger says, "Healthy relationships are built on a foundation of positive emotional experiences and connections. You have an internal set of expectations and preferences regarding your connections with others that guide your behavior. **The more confident in your belief that you are able to create healthy relationships, the less likely you are to experience the kind of avoidance and anxiety that characterizes a damaged belief system.** By creating and strengthening your beliefs and attitudes toward connectedness, you will experience a deeper, more satisfying life."[7]

Sheri and Greg were unable to move through the deepening phase of their relationship because they each had limiting beliefs and patterns of behavior that the other could not tolerate. When they committed to resolving their own issues, their ability to create a meaningful relationship became possible.

> *"There is no mistaking love. You feel it in your heart. It is the common fiber of life, the flame that heats our soul, energizes our spirit and supplies passion to our lives. It is our connection to God and to each other."*
>
> *Elizabeth Kubler-Ross*

Take Action

Consider where you are in the development of key relationships in your life.

1. Have you met someone recently, made an **acquaintance,** that you want to take time to know better? Write his or her name down and make specific times to discover what it is you find interesting about this person. There may be a deeper purpose as to why this person has shown up at this time in your life.
2. Who is in your life now that you are getting to know as a **casual friend**? Decide who on this list builds you up and encourages your heart, and who on this list leaves you feeling smaller. Be intentional about who you choose to allow to get closer and who is not allowed in where you are vulnerable. Casual relationships are important. Most of your friends, business associates, and even certain family members will stay in this list indefinitely.
3. Who are you pursuing a **close or intimate relationship** with? This list will vary in size for different people based on temperament. It should be a very small group, as closeness suggests exclusivity and creates more responsibility.
4. What relationships are **troubled** because of a lack of time or attention? Does a particular friendship or partnership suffer from a lack of clear communication? Do you have a relationship that needs clearer, firmer boundaries? Do you need to make things right with someone by apologizing because of a failure on your part? Do you need to confront someone about how

he or she has hurt you? Relationships do not end by accident but by choice or neglect.

5. What relationships are you allowing to come to an **ending**? As relationships deepen, there is greater vulnerability and the chance that behaviors and beliefs will be exposed that make the person less attractive.

There might be differences in philosophies or standards of behavior. At this point, the issue of commitment becomes very important. A fully committed relationship means you work to resolve issues and negotiate differences. There are times where one partner is unable to maintain that commitment and the relationship comes to an end. Don't let a relationship end due to deterioration, end it intentionally. Know why you are ending it, and end without anger or bitterness.

Some relationships need to come to an end. If you are in a destructive or demeaning relationship, consider getting counseling individually and together. This is just as true for business partnerships as for marriages or close friendships. There is a season to begin, a time to maintain, and then a place where endings occur. Know when it is time to close a door and welcome the opening that is coming. The close relationships in your life should be a source of growth, not destruction. There are few joys in life greater than a healthy, mutually beneficial relationship.

Sheri and Greg's relationship had begun to deteriorate as destructive beliefs and behaviors were exposed. The faulty beliefs running through Sheri and Greg's minds were:

- I can't trust him / her.
- I am going to get hurt again.
- I don't deserve anything better.
- I'm being too picky.
- We don't have enough in common.
- We are too much alike.
- So many relationships fail why should mine be any different?

These beliefs and others were smothering the loving respect trying to blossom in Sheri and Greg's relationship. Focusing on what they wanted and taking active steps toward creating it made it possible to reconnect and begin building on a stronger foundation.

> *"A loyal friend and partner is a powerful defense:*
> *Whoever finds one has found a true treasure.*
> *A loyal friend and partner is beyond price,*
> *There is no measuring his or her worth.*
> *A loyal friend and partner is the elixir of life,*
> *Those who fear Jehovah will find one."*
>
> *Ecclesiastes 6*

When we think of connectedness, our relationships with others are the first that come to mind. We need relationships with others, but also need to have a connection with ourselves: body, soul, and spirit.

> *"The extent to which two people in a relationship can bring up and resolve issues is a critical marker of the soundness of a relationship."*
>
> *Henry Cloud*

Connectedness and Boundaries

It may seem strange that one of the keys to connectedness is creating and maintaining healthy boundaries. Boundaries are dividing lines between you and everything and everyone that is not you. It may seem that these dividing lines would create a wedge, but healthy boundaries offer clarity on responsibilities and responses. Without boundaries, you have chaos and manipulation. With poor boundaries you find yourself saying "yes" to what you don't want and "no" to what you do.[8] It's absolutely true: every relationship you have will improve or derail depending on whether you keep boundaries in place.

You need to develop and maintain healthy boundaries:

- With Others
- With Yourself
- With Your God

Boundaries With Others

What are the beliefs getting in the way of healthy boundaries with others? If you struggle with this you probably hear yourself thinking along these lines:

- I need to keep everyone happy.
- I am just being selfish by not wanting to do what they want.
- I don't want him/her to be mad at me.
- I can probably talk (read manipulate) them into doing what I want.
- They are never available to listen to or go with me.
- It's so much work trying to collaborate. I'll just do it myself.

When we fail to create and maintain healthy boundaries with others we often find ourselves scrambling to please everyone and end up pleasing no one. We feel selfish when we want to say "no", and so we do what we're asked even when it is an imposition or something that will hurt us. There is a constant fear that if we say "no" we will be rejected. The truth is, when we say "no" with respect for ourselves and others we gain respect and appreciation from healthy people. If someone rejects us for telling the truth in a polite, respectful manner about our wants and needs, then we really don't want close relationships with that person anyway.

Another reason we fail to maintain healthy boundaries with others is guilt. If we have failed to follow through or have wronged someone in the past, we will tend to go too far trying to please them and then give out of guilt. We feel we owe it to them to say yes to whatever they want. This happens in parent-child relationships when a parent has not spent enough time with his or her child. It happens in relationships with our parents when we feel we owe a debt of gratitude for all they've done for us. Giving out of love is not the same as caving into inappropriate requests. Finally, we might have trouble saying "no" when someone has suffered. We don't want to add to their grief, so we commit to doing things we are not ready or willing to do. When you have a healthy belief around your ability to connect with others, you are able to maintain boundaries that offer freedom to give out of a loving heart.

When your beliefs support your ability to connect with others, you find people attracted to you in powerful ways. This is because your heart is open and ready to share the gifts, talents and strengths you have within appropriate boundaries.

Boundaries toward Yourself

- If you struggle in the area of boundaries with yourself you might be thinking:
- What I think or do doesn't matter.
- I don't have much to offer.
- My time/possessions/ideas aren't very valuable.
- It doesn't matter if I give in and overeat/overspend/oversleep this once.
- No one is watching; I can get away with it this once.
- I am not enough. I need a (partner/spouse/client) to complete me.

When we fail to create and follow through with boundaries for ourselves, we spiral into devastating patterns of self-sabotage. We become our own worst enemy. Shifting the pattern begins with believing you are worthy of something far better.

All too often we agree to rules or standards for our lives based on what others think we ought to be doing. These rules may or may not be good for us, but we embrace these standards and start out planning to comply. A rule like when to go to bed, when to get up, how often you vacuum your floors, how you spend your money, or whether or not you eat ice cream is sometimes accepted without considering your personal wants and needs. Because the standards were not your own to begin with, you have trouble following through on them. Commitments should be carefully considered based on the desires of your heart. In Chapter 9, a framework is described for making decisions and commitments based on choosing in favor of your passion. We make better choices when we are clear on who we are and what we want.

A special note to victims of trauma or abuse: Don't be surprised if you find yourself struggling with boundaries toward yourself if you were victimized as a child. A high percentage of victims of sexual abuse have struggles with food and money. This is because victims have had their boundaries violated and their sense of self has been damaged. This is especially true if the perpetrator was someone who should have been teaching you good boundaries (like parents, teachers, priests, etc.). Acknowledging the past and determining to rebuild resilience is the first step toward creating healthy boundaries for you and your life. As you become more resilient, you will be able to connect with yourself and follow through on the standards you have set for your life.

A healthy connection with yourself means you respect yourself, have high standards, and treat yourself with kindness. It also means you expect to be treated the same way by others. You enjoy your own company, nurture yourself, and give yourself permission to enjoy the things you enjoy. You expect yourself to succeed because you recognize you were designed for a life of purpose and passion.

Boundaries with Your God

Those who struggle in the area of boundaries with God might think:

- I can make my own rules.
- I feel like I'm being led this way, but I'm going to go another route because (it's easier/others are going that way/etc.).
- I can't be angry at God.
- God isn't treating me the way I want.
- I don't need God in my life.
- My existence has no purpose.

I believe in an Inner Guidance that I call God / Spirit / Father / Christ. You may call it something else, but there is no denying that it is there. The Source of All That Is leads you through your heart. That Voice gives you direction on who you are and what you need to do to fulfill the destiny for which you were designed. Becoming quiet enough to hear that guidance is hard, especially when the noisy wounds of the past and the busyness of daily life get in the way. It is also hard to pay attention to that Voice when expectations have been disappointed. If you were expecting an answer to prayer, an open door, or some gift to come your way and it didn't happen, you might be tempted to harden your heart and stop listening. The problem is you were counting on things that were never promised. God's gifts are perfectly timed and expertly suited to you and your needs. By being so focused on the gift you were expecting, you have missed out on the gift you need. It's like a child who wants a pony for her birthday. She expectantly waits for the pony, and fails to see the beautiful bicycle delivered at her door. She thought she wanted a pony, but she doesn't have the resources or even the interest in taking care of one. But a bicycle meets her needs and offers her fun and freedom without the responsibilities of caring for and feeding a horse.

Here is a story that illustrates this well.

> A terrible flood ravaged a small town. To escape the water crashing through the streets, an old man climbed up on his roof.
>
> "Please God, save me!" he prayed. Shortly after he prayed a state trooper drove up to his house in a Jeep.
>
> "Come down, I'll drive you to safety "the trooper said.
>
> "No thanks—God will save me," the man called out. The waters began to rise, but later a boat filled with people who had been rescued came to the house.

> "Come down, there's room in the boat. We'll take you to safety," called the driver of the boat.
>
> "No thanks—God will save me," the man called out. The waters continued to rise, but soon a Coast Guard helicopter flew over the man's house and dropped a ladder down to the roof.
>
> "Climb the ladder and let us take you to safety!" the officer yelled to the man.
>
> "No thanks—God will save me," the man called out. The waters continued to rise, and eventually the man was swept away and drowned.
>
> When he entered heaven he was angry and demanded an audience with God.
>
> "I prayed and asked You to save me. Where were You when I needed You?" the man cried with a crooked finger pointed at God. God sadly shook His head and answered,
>
> "I don't understand. I sent you a Jeep, a boat and a helicopter—what more did you want?"

Watch for the ways the Spirit of God is leading and directing you. Listen for the rules and standards you are being called to live by. Determine to follow that guidance, no matter what. You will not be disappointed.

> *To be closer to God, be closer to people.*
>
> *Kahlil Gibran*

Marcy's Story

You met Marcy in Chapter 3, and read about the challenging relationships she had with her father, her ex-husband, her children and her customers. Marcy had a hard time with boundaries. She was raised to believe that she had to put herself and her feelings last if she wanted to prove she was a good person. Marcy would avoid conflict at all costs. Keeping the peace meant keeping silent when someone treated her unfairly or demanded more than she wanted to give. Marcy worked hard on rebuilding resilience and came to recognize that when she set limits and established boundaries she strengthened her relationships and made life much easier.

Marcy surprised me one day when she told me about a boundary she set. Every other weekend, her ex-husband came to her house to pick up their children. He would drive up into her driveway behind her car, park, and walk into Marcy's home. Marcy was raising their four busy children while building her own business, so the house is not always as tidy as she would like. From the moment he walked in the door, her ex-husband would begin to criticize Marcy, her house-keeping, her business, and her parenting. He did this in front of the children. Marcy tolerated this for years. It made her angry, but she believed that she deserved the criticism because the house wasn't perfect and she wasn't a perfect parent. It also made Marcy angry that her car was blocked behind her ex-husband's truck. She had to wait for him to get the children loaded into his car and leave before she could take off for her appointments. She didn't mention it, but I believe it also made her very angry that her ex-husband was walking into her home without invitation or permission. She didn't want trouble or conflict in front of her kids, so week after week Marcy put up with his obnoxious behavior.

That all changed when a more resilient Marcy realized she deserved respect. One Saturday morning, Marcy was waiting for her ex-husband in the driveway of her home. He started to pull into the drive, but she waved him to park in the street in front of her house. She then went to the door and waited for him. When he came to the door, Marcy quietly told him this:

> "I have a right to feel safe in my own home. When you block my car in the driveway, I feel trapped. When you come into my home and criticize me in front of our children, I don't feel respected or safe. You are no longer welcome in my home. When you come to pick up the children I expect you to wait for them in your car on the street in front of the house."

Without waiting for a response, Marcy went into her house and gently shut the door. I wish I could have seen the ex-husband's face, don't you?

Later the ex-husband called and complained. He complained to Marcy's parents and friends. He asked the children about these new rules. But in the end, he complied with Marcy's boundaries. Marcy had been afraid of rocking the boat or causing conflict, but the outcome was worth it. Marcy's son began treating her with more respect. Her brother-in-law laughed with her about her new rules and told her she was smart. Her parents did not say one word of recrimination. Marcy found a new respect for herself. She proved to herself that boundaries work.

Vicky's Story

Vicky was sick and tired of having to do it all. She was sick of having to nag her husband into doing anything around the house. She was tired of arguing with her daughter about discipline every time she babysat her grandchildren. She was sick and tired of community volunteers on her committee failing to show up and get the job done. Vicky had another type of boundary problem. In her relationships, Vicky was often controlling and manipulative. You couldn't tell her that though, not without getting an earful of all she had done and was doing for everyone else.

Vicky was smart, efficient, and a go-getter. But Vicky's relationships were filled with tension and unresolved conflicts. What Vicky needed to realize was that in order to create healthy connections, you must respect the boundaries of others. If her husband wanted to nap on a Sunday afternoon, she needed to respect his wish and negotiate later for a time to work on household projects. If her daughter decided to use "time outs" instead of spanking her children, Vicky needed to respect her daughter's position of authority over her children. If a volunteer said "No, I'm sorry I can't make it," then Vicky would get a lot more help later if she respected their decision and not try to talk them into doing things her way.

Vicky grew up with two younger brothers and a mother sick with fibromyalgia. At an early age Vicky took charge of the household and found she felt most secure when she was in control. This pattern took root and governed her relationships as an adult. Learning to hear, receive and respect the word "no" was a huge challenge for Vicky, but when she realized how important it was to her relationships, she did it. And she found something interesting. Once she stopped nagging her husband, he began setting aside time to work around the house. Once she stopped pushing her opinions about child-rearing, her daughter actually began asking for them. Once she stopped ruling her committee with an iron fist, she found more people were willing to join forces and work together. Vicky needed to believe that she could trust the people around her to make good choices. She needed to recognize that whether they made those choices or not was not her concern. Vicky needed to focus on controlling herself and let everyone else take responsibility for their own choices. Life is a lot easier when boundaries and connections are built on trust and respect.

> *"Actions speak louder than words. Businesses must act. Once the door to social consciousness is opened, bring the spirit of your company through it to affect change."*
>
> —*Brian Solis*

Connectedness at Work

Beliefs around connectedness affect every area of life, including the relationships we have at work. Five specific belief barriers are particularly destructive: defensiveness, comparisons, the fraud factor, distractions, and misaligned values. Unless challenged, these belief barriers can disrupt a team and even derail a business.

1. Defensiveness

We are defensive when we have unresolved conflicts and unhealed wounds from past connections with others, and this defensiveness carries over into our work relationships. As we discussed in Chapter 3, a false sense of self-preservation drives us to put up walls to prevent new hurts before they happen. Defensive people see slights and condemnation where there are none and tend to exaggerate any that are real. A defensive posture at work can affect you in several ways. It could mean not volunteering for new, challenging assignments. It could prevent you from receiving constructive criticism or owning your mistakes. It might keep you from asking for help when you need it. There is usually enough stress at work and no one wants to have it intensified by a team member who is defensive and unreceptive. The best way to release defensiveness is to talk openly about your fears with a trusted confidant who will help you see situations as they really are and hold you accountable for your actions and reactions.

2. Comparisons

Comparisons can be an equally destructive barrier to connection. It is human nature to notice the differences among your colleagues. We all have our differences, strengths and weaknesses. The danger comes when someone fails to meet an unwritten standard or criterion. Diversity can be divisive or add variety and spice. Thinking "you're not like me" or "I'm not like them" can be the beginning of a belief that either weakens or builds a connection. Your thinking can take two potential routes:

> "I'm not like them, so I don't belong and never will." or
> "I'm not like them, I can contribute my unique strengths and perspectives."

Personal preferences can be a belief barrier to creating healthy connections. Certain personality types need more time and space than others. Some people need time to consider ideas and how to respond. They may have a greater need for quiet. Other temperaments require more interaction and spontaneity. Those with a more grounded, analytical view might look at abstract thinkers as out of touch or too caught up in possibilities rather than in realities. Personality clashes create serious tension in the workplace. That tension comes when you believe that certain temperaments are robbing you of what you need to function, whether it is time, freedom, space, structure or open-mindedness. This belief will limit your ability to contribute your strengths and talents to your team. The best teams are made up of a variety of people with a variety of skills, temperaments and ways of doing things. Embrace diversity!

3. The Fraud Factor

It is surprising when a successful, well-respected person admits to feeling like a fraud, but it is not uncommon. The Fraud Factor shows up when someone believes he or she must cover up real or imagined faults. The pressure of always needing to appear at your best can lead you to creating an external persona you end up despising. That persona is not real. Lack of authenticity is actually a lack of integrity. It frequently is paired with perfectionism. When a member of a team puts on a front, the rest of the group usually senses it on an unconscious level. Transparency about your personal strengths and weaknesses is the best way to build trust, an essential component of relationships. Transparency requires a certain degree of vulnerability, and vulnerability is a way to create a heart connection with your colleagues.

4. Distractions

Distractions take our focus off the priorities important to the team. Every team has values, goals, agendas, and ideas whether they have been clearly communicated or not. When one member is distracted by conflicting activities, the relationship suffers. Believing in the vision of the team requires vigilant focus as well as the willingness to sacrifice personal agendas. To increase focus, get clear on the expected outcomes and use tools to keep you moving forward, taking action steps to accomplish those objectives.

5. Misaligned Values

When you join a team, you bring your own set of values and principles. Whether or not your company or team has identified core values, they are there. Core values are the reasons things are done the way they are. A value of respect for others will govern how employees and customers are treated. A value of loyalty will prevent gossip, will make sure that credit is given where it is due, and will build customer relationships. A value of quality will ensure a clean work space, a commitment to getting the job done right, and the delivery of excellent service. Connecting with your team will require that you embrace those common values. Communication is much simpler when your personal values match or are aligned with your team. Conversations around values should occur early and often.[9]

Ending Assumptions

Creating connections at work means learning how to communicate with one another and making a commitment to honor that relationship. That means asking instead of assuming. When I work with a company on strategic planning, I often use an exercise that is one of my favorites because it is so eye opening. It involves having everyone write down five specific tasks they do regularly in their job that they love—things that make coming to work fun, exciting and worthwhile. I also ask everyone to write down five things they are required to do in their job that they absolutely hate. These are the things that wear them down, might make them think about working somewhere else, or that they put off as long as they can. If possible, I have a different color of sticky note for each person. Once the notes are written the second phase of the exercise begins. All 10 items written on the sticky notes are posted on a board in front of the room that is divided into two columns: "Love it" and "Loathe it." (Thanks to Marcus Buckingham for this language!)[10] When they put their notes on the board, each team member is given the chance to explain why they love the five things they are posting. It is tremendously eye-opening to hear what ignites passion in your teammates. It is equally eye-opening when we get to the third phase of this exercise. The notes in the "Loathe it" column are read aloud and offered up for adoption. What one member of the team loathes, another team member might find simple or enjoyable. Nearly every time I've done this exercise I've heard gasps of "Really?" or "Are you sure?" as people see tasks they dislike being taken off their shoulders. Occasionally tasks are left on the board because no one wants to do them. This is eye-opening as well, and gives teams and their managers an opportunity to brain storm on how that task might be done differently and more easily.

We tend to think we know our colleagues, what they do well and what they enjoy. I will never forget when years ago a coworker complimented me in a team meeting on my ability to create and use Excel spreadsheets to manage projects. She saw me as being very detail oriented and structured. I nearly laughed out loud. I hate using Excel. And I use it only because I don't track details well and need lots of help with structure. When I shared this with my team, we started a conversation that was very meaningful and productive. We got to really know one another and were better able to support each other in getting our jobs done well.

If your team could benefit from letting go of a few assumptions, I suggest having conversations that include these questions:

- What is the one thing I can always turn to you for?
- What is the best way to communicate with you on a project?
- What is one thing I should never ask you to do?

The answers to these questions will lead to more authenticity, transparency and collaboration on your team.

Taking it deeper

> *"I think people don't feel that they have permission to talk about something that makes them as vulnerable as love, so we don't usually talk about it in public. I once had the idea of having a red bench in every corporation. And the red bench would be an invitation to conversations that matter. So if you sat on the red bench, you were saying, I'm open to a conversation about love, or a conversation about truth, or something that matters to me."*
>
> *Betty Sue Flowers*

When I first discovered the quote above I wondered if the red bench could be something more portable, like carrying a red book to place on a park bench, a church pew, or on the table across from you in a coffee shop. What would it look like it we had meaningful conversations in the workplace on a regular basis? I wonder if meaningful conversations are possible in a world where we hide behind topics like the weather or sports or business as usual. Our souls hunger for conversations that matter. I challenge you to start one and see what happens.

Keys to Creating Connectedness

Creating connectedness is not about leaning forward, hanging on or pushing through. Connectedness comes when we lean back, open up and hold space for someone's heart. The five senses were designed to take information in, to be receptive. They do not push information forward. The same is true of the heart. It is emotionally receptive. **Once you have rebuilt resilience and established healthy boundaries you are ready to open your heart to receive and respond with compassion, vulnerability, and authenticity.** We have become so afraid of harm in our society that we are guarded against this type of openness. In order to keep your heart open, there are three things to consider:

First, take time to connect with your own heart. Take inventory of feelings you find there and resolve to put any issues of anger or bitterness away. Anger and bitterness are like concrete walls embedded with shards of glass designed to keep others away. Forgiveness does not mean forgetting the harm that created those feelings of anger, but it means putting the anger aside and making a conscious choice not to hold the harm against the people who hurt you. You let go of the ties you've bound yourself with to the one who harmed you, and free yourself to live without bitterness. This letting go is an act of the will and it will need to be repeated again and again depending on how deeply you've been hurt.

Once you've freed yourself from the bonds of bitterness, you want to ask yourself if you want to choose to connect. Love is a choice. Connectedness needs to come from a conscious decision and not be based on fleeting feelings of attraction or interest. We make non-verbal commitments to others when we let them in our hearts. We need to be sure we have the emotional energy to fulfill our responsibilities in the relationship.

When I began to consider the possibility that I might get married again, it required a conscious choice to open my heart to the possibility of love, vulnerability and transparency. I had been deeply hurt in my first marriage, and the choice to open my heart did not come easily. I had to practice forgiveness and letting go of anger and bitterness daily for years before I was ready to move forward. The decision to open your heart does not come with any guarantees. You risk being hurt again, but that risk is part of what makes new relationships so exciting. Knowing your own heart and preparing to share it is an essential part of connectedness.

Next, **you want to make a conscious choice about who you want to connect with** and know his or her heart. This is true whether you are considering a romantic relationship or a business partnership. Focus on what you know about this person and what your spirit or intuition tells you. Listen to your gut. The more you tune into your intuition, the more you find yourself to be a good judge of character. Your mind will tell you what you see on the surface, the evidence of how they live their life. Your spirit will tell you what cannot be seen, the truth of why they live the way they do. Be aware of any check in your spirit, that sense that something isn't all it should be. If there is a question, get answers. If there is doubt, ask yourself if it is based on fear or truth.

I made a drastic mistake when I married the first time. I thought I knew my fiancé since we had dated for nearly three years. But there was something not quite right about him. On the surface he was attractive, well educated, had a good job and attended the same church I did. Underneath it all, though, there was something hidden from view. Six weeks before our wedding, I seriously considered calling it off. I consulted with my pastor, my parents and friends. Everyone told me I was just having "wedding jitters." The one person I did not talk to was my fiancé. I went ahead against my intuition and got married. What a mistake! I discovered on my honeymoon that my husband was mentally ill. He had been able to hide this from me until the closeness and intimacy of marriage caused his issues to explode into full view. I'll never know what my life would have been without that mistake. I know I learned a great deal and would not be who I am today without those lessons. One of the most important lessons: Listen to your heart and make conscious choices based on what it tells you.

The final step in creating connectedness is to **commit to serving those you have chosen to connect with.** In another time, commitments to connect were seen as binding pledges, promises of obligation, dedication of loyalty, vows and promises. Today our view of commitment has eroded and we see our obligation as applying more to what is convenient. The key to creating connectedness is a willingness to commit without reservation with the view that you are in it to give, not take.[11] You can receive what your partner has to give with joy, but you do not take with a sense of entitlement or expectation. When good comes your way, you receive it with joy and gratitude. When something you need or want does not come, you check your heart to see if that need or want is supposed to come from another source. But in all of this is the commitment to invest yourself and all you can bring to the relationship.

- Your acquaintance receives your commitment to be a man or woman who lives their values with full integrity.
- Your casual friend receives your commitment of being fully present when you are together.

- Your business partner receives your commitment to bring your best all the time.
- Your close friend receives your commitment to hear their heart's secrets with honesty and loyalty.
- Your spouse receives your commitment to faithfulness in morality, finances, and devotion.
- Your God receives your commitment to fulfill the purpose for which you were designed.

I know personally as a divorced person that there are times when relationships and commitments must end. But I also know how easily we are tempted to walk away in today's culture. I can say without any shame that I was fully committed to my marriage until it came time to leave. Some urged me to leave my marriage sooner; others continue to condemn my decision to divorce. I'm the only one who knew when it was the right time to walk away.

I also know as a businesswoman that not all business partnerships should last forever. There needs to be a plan in place for how a business partnership will be dissolved before the formal relationship ever begins.

I know that friendships end.

In all these cases, a relationship never needs to be ended in anger. Even if one party has wronged the other, resolve the conflicts as best you can and then let go. In this you fulfill your commitment to serve as you honor yourself and the person with whom you were connected.

> *"Strange is our situation here upon earth. Each of us comes for a short visit, not knowing why, yet sometimes seeming to a divine purpose. From the standpoint of daily life, however, there is one thing we do know: That we are here for the sake of others . . . for the countless unknown souls with whose fate we are connected by a bond of sympathy. Many times a day, I realize how much my outer and inner life is built upon the labors of people, both living and dead, and how earnestly I must exert myself in order to give in return as much as I have received."*
>
> *Albert Einstein*

EXERCISES for Creating Connectedness

1. Active Listening Exercise

Active listening involves taking in what another person is saying without judgment or assumption. In this exercise one person tells a story about something that happened to him or her personally, e.g., an embarrassing moment. The other person listens attentively, leans forward, makes good eye contact and nods encouragingly. When the storyteller is finished, the listener then repeats what they heard as exactly as possible. The listener may paraphrase and should attempt to capture the meaning and emotion behind the words. The storyteller then gives feedback on how well the listener did and how it feels to be heard this way. The storyteller and the listener then trade roles and begin again.

2. Heart Talk Exercise

A heart talk takes place in a small group or family. The group agrees to the following:

One person is given a heart to hold and begins speaking. No one speaks unless they are holding the heart. The speaker talks about how they feel about a situation in the group. No judging or criticizing is allowed. Once the speaker is finished, he or she passes the heart to the left and the next person begins speaking. Anything said during a Heart Talk is kept confidential. The members of the group agree not to leave until everyone has spoken or the exercise is declared complete.

The results of a Heart Talk Exercise are enhanced listening, constructive expression of feelings, improved conflict resolution, improved abilities to let go of resentments and old issues, the development of mutual respect, and a greater sense of connection to the group.

3. Speak with Impeccability

Based on *The Four Agreements* by Don Miguel Ruiz, this exercise is designed to help you master your tongue, tell the truth and avoid gossip.[12]

Find an accountability partner and set a specific period of time to focus on Speaking with Impeccability. The time can be as short as an hour or as long as a week. During that time, keep track of every instance in which you spoke anything less than the truth or any type of gossip. At the end of the time period, report back to your accountability partner and reveal what your underlying emotions and motives were when you failed to speak with impeccability. Look within to see what needs you have that are driving your speech. Reward yourself in some way every time you were able to avoid lies or gossip. Monitor your progress and watch your speech improve.

4. Express Appreciation

Mother Theresa of Calcutta said "There is more hunger for love and appreciation in this world than for bread." For this exercise, find unique ways to express appreciation using all modalities: Auditory, Visual, and Kinesthetic. Auditory appreciation (something the person can hear) might seem simple, unless you get creative and make the appreciation musical. Visual appreciation (something the person can see) could be a card, letter, or a clean car. Kinesthetic appreciation (something the person can feel) could be a hug, a dance, or a game of catch. Get creative!

5. Ask for Criticism

Learn to eliminate defensiveness by asking for and receiving constructive criticism. Start with someone you trust to be gentle and ask them for feedback on something you could improve. Thank the person for their feedback and then go somewhere quiet. Take the criticism in and ask yourself:

- Do I trust this person to be fair?
- Do I believe the criticism is accurate?
- Do I know what I need to do to improve?
- What am I feeling? What will I do to resolve negative feelings?
- What are my next steps?

6. Rate your Relationships

You were encouraged to take action and rate each of your key relationships on where they are developmentally. Do this now and with each one ask yourself, is this relationship I want? Is it:

- Beginning
- Building
- Deepening
- Deteriorating
- Terminating

7. Test Your Boundaries

In the section on boundaries, a list of possible false beliefs was listed. Read through each statement, find the lie, and change the sentence to make it true and how you will make it true.

- Boundaries With Others
    - I need to keep everyone happy.
        - Example: I don't need to keep everyone happy. Everyone is responsible for his or her own happiness. I allow them to find joy without inserting myself.
    - I am just being selfish by not wanting to do what they want.
    - I don't want him/her to be mad at me.
    - I can probably talk (read manipulate) them into doing what I want.
    - They are never available to listen to or go with me
    - It's so much work trying to collaborate. I'll just do it myself.

- Boundaries With Yourself
    - What I think doesn't matter.
    - What I'm doing isn't all that important.

    - I don't have much to offer.
    - My time/possessions/ideas aren't very valuable.
    - It doesn't matter if I give in and overeat/overspend/oversleep this once.
    - No one is watching, I can get away with it this once.
    - I am not enough. I need a (partner/spouse/client) to complete me.

- Boundaries With Your God
    - I can make my own rules.
    - I feel like I'm being led this way, but I'm going to go another route because (it's easier/others are going that way/etc.).
    - I can't be angry at God.
    - God isn't treating me the way I want.
    - I don't need God in my life.
    - There is no purpose for my existence.

8. End Your Assumptions

Meet with a colleague or co-worker and ask him or her the following:

- What is the one thing I can always turn to you for?
- What is the best way to communicate with you on a project?
- What is one thing I should never ask you to do?

9. Solidify Your Commitments

In the section "Keys to Creating Connection," a list of relationships and the commitments made to each are listed. What are the commitments you are making in your relationships?

- Your acquaintance receives your commitment to ____.

- Your casual friend receives your commitment to
  ____.

- Your business partner receives your commitment to
  ____.

- Your close friend receives your commitment to
  ____.

- Your spouse receives your commitment to
  ____.

- Your God receives your commitment to
  ____.

CHAPTER 5

INCREASING INITIATIVE

Initiative [ih-**nish**-ee-*uh*-tiv] The power or ability to begin or to follow through energetically with a plan or task.

"Success comes from taking the initiative and following up . . . persisting . . . eloquently expressing the depth of your love. What simple action could you take today to produce a new momentum toward success in your life?"
Anthony Robbins

When was the last time you struggled to get started on a task? How often do you find yourself putting something off until it is almost embarrassing? You wait for the right timing, the right people, the right formation of the papers on your desk, and even for the stars to align and say "Go!" Or maybe you find yourself so caught up in a project that you neglect your family, friends and other responsibilities. Your problem is not getting started; you can't seem to stop until the whole, huge thing is done. All these issues relate to your beliefs around initiative.

Initiative is the ability to begin or to follow through energetically with a plan or task; it includes enterprise and determination. Initiative is the power to assess and take action independently. Initiative is an essential ingredient in success, but as a character quality is easily misunderstood. Many think that initiative is based on pure self-discipline, that sheer effort will push you through to your goals. Discipline will help you keep moving forward, but few people have the willpower to force themselves to get up, keep moving, and take action. Many quit before they have hardly begun, because they believe the task is too hard, the effort will take too long, and they know they don't have enough will power to complete the task. They wonder how others get so far and wonder what is missing in their character that keeps them from getting where they want to go. But initiative is *not* just self-discipline. **Initiative is the result of passion, purposeful planning, and clarity on your ideal life and work.**

Liv had set the alarm for 5:30 AM, because she had every intention of going for a walk first thing in the morning. She needed the exercise. But when the alarm went off, she rolled over and went back to sleep. She was too tired because she had stayed up reading much later than she should have. Liv dragged herself out of bed and wandered into the kitchen. She needed to make herself a healthy breakfast to fuel her morning, but settled for tea and toast. After spending more time than she'd planned on the newspaper, she booted up her computer. She had told her assistant that she would have the copy for her newsletter done by noon today but she hasn't even started it yet. She opened up Facebook and spent an hour there under the auspices of keeping connected with her clients and customers. What she was really doing was watching videos and commenting on posts that had nothing to do with her work. E-mail captured another hour, and before Liv ever got started on her article it was nearly time for lunch. 'Oh well,' she shrugged, 'I will get the article done after I take a quick break.'

Liv had serious issues around initiative because of limiting beliefs about self-discipline and about what it takes to be truly successful. She had a deep-seated fear of failure. Unless Liv was 100% sure she could do something well, she wouldn't even start. Liv also had health issues that frequently caused low energy and lack of focus. A lack of clarity around her vision scattered her efforts, making progress toward her goals erratic at best. When Liv got into a project, there was no stopping her. The problem was she often under-estimated the time a task required and would not want to stop until it was done. That over-focus created conflict with friends and family.

What is surprising is that Liv is not someone most people would call an apathetic slacker. As a self-employed business woman she had a reputation for good work and solid results. But Liv was never going to experience the kind of success and satisfaction she wanted unless something changed. I know, because LIV stands for Lisa Isobel Van Allen.

Of the seven beliefs described in this book, initiative is the one I personally wrestle with the most. I've had to work on each of the beliefs, but initiative is the one belief I make a conscious effort on every day. Finding the balance point between apathy and being consumed by a task does not come naturally to me. But I am no longer the woman in the paragraph above. Let me tell you what I have learned about belief barriers to initiative and how to overcome them.

Initiative and Guilt

People who struggle with initiative will usually find its roots in early childhood. In his book *Childhood and Society,* Erik Erikson outlined several phases of development, including "Initiative vs. Guilt." This phase covered the preschool years (ages 3-6) during which children learn to make their own decisions and take action on those choices.[1] Guilt is the result of poor choices or outcomes. Erikson believed that children could overcome this guilt if and when they felt a sense of accomplishment. However, young children who are not allowed to make their own choices and are criticized for their actions develop skewed beliefs about their ability to take successful action. They develop doubts and fears that lead to perfectionism, a tendency to overwork, and even apathy if their efforts are rewarded with immediate success. During this critical phase we learn we can master our environment with small successes that lead to achievement. If this lesson is not learned, a false sense of guilt can create feelings of embarrassment. Feelings of guilt and shame can also cause people to become over-dependent on others as they doubt their own abilities.

A realistic assessment of your skills coupled with a determination to overcome these entrenched beliefs is the only way to eliminate this pattern of behavior. You may need to have an objective party give you honest feedback about your work and your abilities. Asking for this assessment feels like a huge risk when your confidence is low, but you will find such relief when you have evidence that you can take empowered action. I highly recommend tools like Strengthsfinder 2.0[2], the Myers-Briggs Type Indicator[3], the Hogan Personality Inventory[4] and similar assessments to give you a more accurate evaluation of your unique gifts.

> *"Inaction breeds doubt and fear. Action breeds confidence and courage. If you want to conquer fear, do not sit home and think about it. Go out and get busy."*
>
> *Dale Carnegie*

10 Keys to Increasing Initiative

Marcy had started her home-based craft business to have the flexibility she needed to stay at home with her children. After struggling to build her business for several years, Marcy found that the work she had been doing to build better beliefs was finally paying off. With better boundaries, Marcy raised her prices, established policies and procedures and became so successful that she was able to move her business to a studio. When she first started her business, Marcy ran on fear. She knew she had to succeed to feed her kids and pay her rent. She was afraid of failing, and so she worked long and hard to become recognized for her talent and skill. The newness of the studio and the excitement of unexpected opportunities added life to her work for a while. She put in long hours for the sheer joy of being a successful business owner in her new space. But after a few months, the newness had worn off, the bills began to come in, and fear began to paralyze

Marcy's efforts. At this point Marcy and I had a conversation analyzing her work flow and trying to determine just why she was so discouraged in spite of her earlier successes.

One of Marcy's most popular products required a great deal of time and attention to create. It was hand crafted and the most expensive item in her line. During a coaching session a few months after renting her studio, Marcy began (in her words) to whine about having to work on this time-consuming project day after day. She began talking about leaving her business for a completely new venture because she didn't believe she had what it took to persist in putting in the time needed to keep her revenue stream moving. Marcy had lost her love for her craft and feared that all her hard work to build her business was for nothing.

This is the point where some would tell Marcy to push through, discipline herself, and get the job done whether she liked it or not. There are several problems with this approach. Marcy did not have a problem with discipline, but with her approach to initiative. Let's take a closer look at what was getting in Marcy's way and the **10 Keys to Increasing Initiative**:

Key #1: **Break large projects into smaller, more management steps.**

Marcy was feeling overwhelmed by a large, tedious project. When she first started her business, she did not have nearly as much pressure or the volume of projects weighing on her. But now she had marketing to plan, accounting to track and this large project to complete. She was running out of steam. She needed to simplify her approach. Task analysis is the process of breaking complex tasks into smaller, more manageable steps. When these simple tasks are completed and combined, they add up to the successful completion a larger, possibly overwhelming project.

Key #2: Create early wins to create confidence.

Marcy needed to see results—the sooner the better. Early wins would help her gain confidence and momentum. When Marcy's focus was on the project as a whole, she missed the pieces she could finish quickly to give her a sense of completion.

Key #3: Mix tedious tasks with more interesting tasks.

Marcy thought that a project wasn't done until the whole thing was completed, but shifting her focus on to sections of the project and creating a plan to break up tedious sections with more interesting tasks gave her renewed energy.

Key #4: Take care of your health before you take care of business to ensure you have the energy and focus needed to complete tasks successfully.

Marcy had been working very hard to get to this point in her business. Her hard work meant long hours, skipping meals or eating unhealthy foods, lack of sleep, and little exercise. She did not have the physical energy to push through and get the job done. Marcy's problem was not one of discipline, but of managing projects in a way that did not sacrifice her health.

Key #5: Sometimes good enough is good enough. Perfectionism is destructive.

Marcy has won awards and built a reputation for excellent work. Her standard of excellence was demanding. A microscopic flaw meant starting over or picking it to death. Marcy needed to learn to see her work through others' eyes and know when it was good enough to be released.

Key #6: Get clear on your strategy and follow through with action.

Marcy had lost sight of her plans to diversify her offerings. There were new items in her product line that were less expensive, and required very little of her time. When she did a little research, she discovered she could automate this process and offer the line to a whole new set of customers. Marcy found a whole new stream of income by following through on her strategic plan.

Key #7: Delegate what you can to others so you can focus on the bigger picture.

Initiative does not mean trying to do it all. Once smaller tasks are identified, it is easier to delegate them to others who can support you in achieving your goals. Marcy had several contract employees, but she was not training or delegating enough work to them.

Key #8: Make time to play. Fun is a brain energizer.

Marcy didn't feel there was anything new, challenging or fun in her work. Joy attracts successful solutions. Marcy needed to make work fun again. She needed to make space to do the things that she loves and does best. Thinking she had to push through and work on tedious projects hour after hour was making her hate her business. Even if deadlines need to be adjusted, making room for healthy play and fun would save her dream in the long run.

Key #9: Know your passion and purpose. Connect everything you do to purpose.

Marcy had let the fire of her passion die. She was feeling so burned out that when a vendor offered her a job, she gave it serious thought. She wasn't sure if she wanted to continue her business. Feeling overwhelmed, Marcy had forgotten why she started her business. Her number one priority was and is her children. She is passionate about spending time with them and being involved in their music and sports activities. A regular job would not allow Marcy the freedom she has a business owner.

Key #10 to: Practice gratitude and abundance will come.

In the middle of overwhelm, Marcy had lost her sense of gratitude and appreciation for all she had. She had a great business with adoring customers. She had a beautiful new studio. She had replaced her nurse's salary with her own business income. She had time for her kids. There was much to be thankful for, and normally Marcy was very grateful. When she counted her blessings, the clouds of doubt and fear began to lift.

By the end of our conversation, Marcy had an action plan she could follow through on that included tasks she enjoyed and tasks she would delegate, marketing efforts that would generate demand for passive income, a plan for breaking tedious work into manageable chunks, and a commitment to take care of her physical needs. Applying the **10 Keys to Increasing Initiative** made taking action feel easy and exciting again. The shift in her attitude was great, but it exploded into joy later that day when she received new orders from new customers. She was ready, equipped with a plan and re-energized passion.

The belief that success is hard work nearly killed Marcy's business. There is a time and place for hard work, but it is simply not true that you have to strive and endure and press through in order to succeed.

"Discipline is the bridge between goals and accomplishments."
Jim Rohn

Daily Acts of Discipline

When you hear the word discipline you might shrink back with feelings of guilt or fear. Most of us feel we need more discipline in our lives. The word discipline originally meant training, but somewhere along the line the concept of punishment was added. A disciple is someone who closely follows the teachings of another, living by a certain code or set of standards. Daily Acts of Discipline are the routines you create to achieve the results you want. They become a part of you. You already have routines you have established as Daily Acts of Discipline, like brushing your teeth or making your bed. I don't know many people who get excited about brushing their teeth (maybe a dentist or two), but we do it as part of our routine. Daily Acts of Discipline are how you create the structure you need to be successful. By failing to create these daily acts, you risk losing the benefits of discipline. You risk making initiative much harder than it needs to be. When I need to create a Daily Act of Discipline, I attach a statement to it that helps me make it part of myself. "This is who I am." I am a woman who brushes her teeth twice a day and makes her bed every morning. I am a woman who strives to eat fresh vegetables every day. I am a woman who gets out and walks early in the morning. I am a woman who writes articles for her business every week. This is who I am.

Who are *you?* What are the behaviors you want and need to make a part of your routine?

To achieve real success, certain behaviors must change. Some changes are easy to make, especially if you experience an immediate reward or benefit. **Daily Acts of Discipline make taking action part of your routine. This routine gives you lots of opportunities to practice the new behaviors you want to adopt. This routine also gives you more opportunities to succeed.** Day in and day out you practice whatever it is you are trying to do. For example, I'm not very fond of exercise. Once I get started I enjoy myself, but there are many things I would rather do than work out. Having a Daily Act of Discipline in which I exercise every day helps me create a routine that gets me out and moving. This routine becomes easier and easier every day, as I create a new habit. I begin to associate this routine with other things. In my case, I associate my daily walk with my husband as time for us to talk, something I do want to do. The act of exercising also gets easier every day, as my body and mind adapt to the new routine. (I'm not nearly as winded at the end of our walk as I was when we first started!)

What does all this have to do with your mindset or belief system? Creating new routines through Daily Acts of Discipline will break down old routines and the beliefs that go with them. Someone who hasn't been exercising regularly may hold the belief that they are old and lazy. **A Daily Act of Discipline shifts negative beliefs and replaces it with a new supportive belief.** That belief might be, "I'm getting stronger every day." There is power in creating new routines, and those routines become even more powerful when you combine them with rewards.

Your brain is wired to look for feedback and reinforcement, particularly when you engage in a new behavior. **The more immediate and meaningful the reward, the more your new behavior is reinforced.** When I started my morning walk routine, I decided to reward myself with time to play a computer game while I enjoy an ice cold protein shake. This simple indulgence will best reinforce my walking if I enjoy it immediately after the walk is done. The farther you are from a reward, the less likely you are to maintain disciplined behavior. Tangible results make taking initiative much easier.

Discipline frequently means saying 'no' to certain things in life. To achieve and maintain a healthy body, you say 'no' to certain foods and sedentary behavior. But this 'no' is actually a 'yes' to the things that take you closer to your goal. Saying no to fatty foods means saying yes to healthier choices like fruits and vegetables. Saying 'no' to time in front of the television is saying 'yes' to taking walks, reading a book, and enjoying time with your family. Here is where another shift in belief occurs: **learning to identify each and every 'yes' that takes you closer to your passion makes every 'no' easier.**

When you are clear on you passion and purpose, taking initiative to live with Daily Acts of Discipline becomes easier. **Every time you are faced with a choice, decision, or opportunity you choose in favor of your passion**. This choice becomes easier as you have more and more clarity. Let's use the example of someone frustrated with dieting to achieve a certain weight. She tries to diet and exercise, but finds herself achieving inconsistent results. Many men and women gain weight when focusing on dieting because they are focused on food, fat, and lack (the food they miss eating). Shifting the focus to what you want, like having a healthy body that looks and feels great, can make your goal more achievable. When you are clear on your passion for looking and feeling great, you will identify the activities that make this passion real in your life. As choices, decisions or opportunities present themselves, you choose in favor of your passion. Every time you open your mouth to eat something, you are faced with a decision. You can ask, "Does this take me closer to my goal or further away?" Every morning, you have a choice to put on your slippers or your tennis shoes. Once you've got those tennis shoes on it is much easier to step out for a walk! It is the small choices we make and the actions we take that create the initiative and discipline required to succeed.

> *"We must not, in trying to think about how we can make a big difference, ignore the small daily differences we can make which, over time, add up to big differences that we often cannot foresee."*
>
> *Marian Wright Edelman*

Motivation

Motivation is the urge to start a task and the energy that carries us through. Motivation is a major factor in increasing initiative, but probably not in the way you think. Many people seem to believe that they are a slave to their level of motivation. They either have it or they don't. This is not true. For centuries we have been taught that we are motivated only to avoid pain or increase pleasure. To increase motivation, you simply had to increase the sense of pain or the possibility of pleasure. But in the last decade Dr. Steven Reiss interviewed over 6,000 people and discovered that the desires that motivate us are much more unique. Reiss identified 16 desires that drive nearly all meaningful behavior. The desires are:

- Power
- Independence
- Curiosity
- Acceptance
- Order
- Status
- Vengeance
- Romance / Sex
- Saving
- Honor
- Idealism
- Social contact
- Family
- Eating
- Physical exercise
- Tranquility[5]

Identifying such a varied list of motivating factors is helpful when we wish to increase our motivation for a challenging task or behavior. As I mentioned above, I tend not to be motivated by physical exercise, but I am highly motivated by acceptance. Recognizing that I will find greater acceptance with my audiences when I show up to speak with a fit and trim body is a motivator to pay better attention to my diet and exercise. Money or status has never been a driving factor in my work, but I am driven by idealism, saving others from self-sabotage, and the power I have to make my business successful.

If one motivator does not work, find one that does.

Richard Ryan and Edward Deci are social psychologists who have researched and written about intrinsic motivation. According to their research, we tend to be personally motivated only by things that interest us, but we can increase our motivation with three powerful factors.

> **Motivation Factor 1**: Our level of motivation increases when we are faced with a challenge. That challenge needs to be something we are fairly certain we can achieve and receive positive feedback.
>
> **Motivation Factor 2**: Personal motivation increases when we have control or the freedom to determine how we are going to reach our goals.
>
> **Motivation Factor 3**: Knowing that other people care about our success and about us personally increases our motivation.

We can motivate ourselves to do what needs to get done. We might not be especially interested in something, but we know that doing it will help us achieve a particular goal. Based on the research above, we can find things that drive us and then add the three motivation factors to increase our interest in doing what needs to be done.

Back to my exercise example: I am not particularly driven to exercise, but I know working out regularly will help me look and feel better. First, I attach my need for exercise with things that do drive me, such as acceptance and idealism. Then I add the three motivation factors:

1—I create a challenging exercise routine that I can achieve (e.g., walking a mile every day) and get good feedback on (e.g., praise and encouragement from my husband);
2—I make sure I control the situation by picking the form of exercise, the time and place, what I wear, etc.; and
3—I find people who genuinely care about my success who will cheer me on (e.g., my mom, my best friend). When the right drivers and the motivation factors are in place, getting things done is much easier.

> *". . . the moment one definitely commits oneself, then Providence moves too. All sorts of things occur to help one that would never otherwise have occurred. A whole stream of events issues from the decision, raising in one's favor all manner of unforeseen incidents and meetings and material assistance, which no man could have dreamed would have come his way. Whatever you can do, or dream you can do, begin it. Boldness has genius, power, and magic in it. Begin it now."*
>
> *Goethe*

Putting POWER behind Initiative

In Chapter 1 you were introduced to the POWER process for setting intentions and taking inspired action. Intentions are meaningless without initiative. Often we are paralyzed by fear of failure and believe that we are incapable of making our dreams come true. We allow our external reality to control our internal experience. Externally we see and hear things that limit our belief that we can take action and be successful. Internally we have a dream or desire that can only become a reality when we take inspired action. Breaking the process into specific action steps will help alleviate the fear. You need POWER.

P— What is the **PROBLEM** I am facing? Another way to say this is: What is my **PURPOSE**?

Define exactly what it is that you want to accomplish. What behavior do you want to change? What obstacle do you want to overcome? What is calling to you? What is your heart's desire? Get completely clear on what you want. Over the years as I've used the POWER process with clients, I have noticed that this was one of the steps people tended to skip. It sounds silly, but people have a tendency to take action before they are clear on what it is they are trying to accomplish. The complaint about men who drive around lost without asking for directions comes to mind. If they were clear on where they were going and the route they were going to take before starting the car, there wouldn't be a problem! But men are not the only ones who jump in without clarity or direction. We all need to define our purpose.

During this phase of the process, it is important to open up to every possibility. Ask for guidance and align your will to the direction and purpose God has for your life. Allow yourself to dream, and then share your dream with others. Martin Luther King, Jr. declared "I have a dream!" and found thousands of others who would support his vision and joined him in taking action. We need this kind of support to bolster our motivation and encourage us when the work gets hard.

O—What are my **options** and **objectives**?

This is another phase in the POWER process that adults tend to want to overlook. Children are great at generating options. They have not closed their minds to possibilities. Look at every alternative and possible way you could achieve your deepest desires. Then create specific markers, goals and objectives that will move you toward your dream. There are differences between these three things. **Markers** are not necessarily measureable, but they are the things that will help you recognize that you are on the right track as you move toward your goal. **Goals** are more abstract and focused on the long term. They are the reason why you want to achieve your vision. **Objectives** are very focused on a shorter span of time and are SMART: specific, measureable, achievable, relevant, and time oriented.

Let's say you have a dream of climbing Mt. Everest. Here are some possible markers, goals, and objectives:

Possible Markers

You are invited to a meeting where someone who has climbed Mt. Everest is speaking and you will get a chance to ask her questions about her trek.

You receive money you weren't expecting that is just enough for airfare to Nepal.

Possible Goals

You want to get into the best physical condition of your life.

You want to write a book about your experience preparing and climbing Mt. Everest that will inspire others to accomplish their goals.

Possible Objectives

You will create a savings account and put $500 a month into it toward your trip expenses

You will join a gym and work 3 times a week with a personal trainer who knows about climbing

You will join an online community of people who climb the highest mountains in the world and discuss climbing with them at least once a week.

As you set your markers, goals, and objectives you will see the process of achieving your dream unfold. Jim Rohn gave great advice on creating goals:

> *"You want to set a goal that is big enough that in the process of achieving it you become someone worth becoming."*

As you identify your markers, goals and objectives, visualize your results. Find ways to keep your vision in front of you. Create vision boards, collages, or boards on Pinterest.com with images that capture the essence of your dream and every step you are taking to make it real. These pictures can be used to visualize yourself doing the very thing you want to achieve. Visualization is a powerful technique. When you visualize yourself doing something, your brain creates neural pathways in the same way as when you actually do it. Mental rehearsal is a technique used by Olympic athletes, public speakers, and other professionals. With established neural pathways, your brain is prepared to help you achieve your objectives.

EXERCISES to Increase Initiative

1. Increasing Initiative in Small Steps

Take out a journal and consider these questions:

- What is a goal that I've had difficulty achieving that would benefit from a routine of Daily Acts of Discipline?
- What routines do I want to establish as Daily Acts of Discipline?
- How do I plan to reward myself when I successfully follow through on my new routine?

2. Create a New Routine

Create an experiment with one simple behavior (i.e., putting on your tennis shoes instead of your slippers) and commit to doing it every day for one week. Track your progress. Do NOT beat yourself up, because initiative and discipline does not need to be fueled by punishment. Instead, shift your focus on what you want and how you plan to get there. For additional help, have someone ask you if you did what you set out to do. Knowing the question is coming will strengthen your motivation. Creating and fulfilling Daily Acts of Discipline will make you more successful in your personal and professional life!

3. Visualization: Ride Thought Waves

Sit quietly in a place where you won't be distracted. Take a few deep breaths to clear your mind. Choose an objective you'd like to visualize. It could be something simple like organizing your desk or something more complicated like switching to a new career. Find a clear, specific, measurable objective, but you don't need a plan of action at this point.

Consider what you want. Imagine your goal becoming real. Let yourself daydream, but stay awake as you do it. Explore the goal in your mind. Picture it actually happening, but don't take any action at this point. For example, if your goal is to switch to a new career, then imagine yourself in that new career right now. Think about what it would be like to actually do that kind of work. Picture yourself doing the work and enjoying it. See the people you're working with, and hold imaginary conversations with them.

Within a few minutes, positive thoughts about your goal will build up so much energy in your body that you'll want to take action. Now it's time to pull out the virtual surfboard and catch the wave. Within a few minutes, you should be noticing different physical sensations in your body – IF your goal is attractive enough to you. Extra blood may even flow to your brain and muscles, preparing you for action. Once you start feeling that positive tension in your body, stop and ask yourself this question:

> What can I do right now to make this goal a reality?
> As you ask this question, hold the expectation that the answer will be something simple that can be done in 30 minutes or less. Whatever reasonable answer pops into your head, accept it and act on it immediately. At this point you should find it very easy to take action.

4. 10 Keys to Increasing Initiative

In your journal, write down the numbers 1 – 10 and create an action step for each of the 10 Keys.

1 – What large project or job needs to be broken into smaller, more manageable chunks?
2 – Which of those chunks would offer you an early win?
3 – What more tedious task do you have that could be broken up with more interesting tasks? How long will you spend on each?
4 – What one area of your health do you tend to neglect? What will you do differently to protect your health and energy?
5 – What is something that you tend to be perfectionistic about? How are you critical of your work? What do you need to do to finish and release this project?
6 – Do you have a plan for what you are trying to do? Is there a specific part of your plan that you've neglected or forgotten?

7 – What tasks do you intend to delegate to others?
8 – What type of fun will you insert into your work?
9 – Look at your action plan and write how each step relates to your purpose. If you have difficulty with this exercise, wait until after reading chapter 9 and then complete it.
10 – What are you grateful for in your work? What about this project are you thankful for?

5. What Drives You?

In the section on Motivation, I listed 16 desires that drive different people. In your journal:

List what drives you:

List what doesn't drive you:

Which drives in your first list can you use to offset the drives in your second list?

6. Motivating Factors

Think of a task you have that you lack motivation for and then consider how you can use the three Motivating Factors to help you get it done:

Challenge:

Control:

Support:

7. POWER

Memorize the POWER acronym and apply it to Increase Initiative:

Problem – Options – Work – Evaluate - Reward

CHAPTER 6

EXPANDING EXCELLENCE

['ek suh luhns] The quality or state of being outstanding or extremely good.

"We are what we repeatedly do.
Excellence, therefore, is not an act but a habit."
Aristotle

Excellence is seen as a requirement for success in today's culture. Somehow to simply do a good job is not enough. Average has been branded as mediocre and very good is barely enough. The problem with this thinking is it creates unrealistic expectations and drives people toward perfectionism. No one can be great at everything all the time. So how does one find balance between mediocrity and perfectionism? How can we be excellent? Comparing ourselves to a certain standard of excellence can be beneficial and challenging in a healthy way. Comparing ourselves to others can be defeating and discouraging. There is a quote that has been floating around social media: "Don't compare someone else's highlight reel to your behind-the-scenes bloopers." You rarely know all the time and effort someone spent in becoming excellent. Usually you only get to see the final outcome of that hard work and preparation. **Excellence is a process of becoming and depends upon a belief that you can keep reaching and growing to achieve your objective.** Excellence is dependent upon focus, practice, and clarity about the goal in mind. It is time to rethink our definitions and rebuild our beliefs around excellence.

Mediocrity

When efforts fall short and are labeled mediocre, it is easy to jump to conclusions. There is an assumption that if we try hard enough, work long enough, and give it our best, it will never fall into that dark hole called mediocrity. The truth is that we all have mediocre moments. These moments make the times we touch excellence shine all the brighter. Sheer effort is not enough to avoid mediocrity. There are beliefs that prevent us from tapping into our brilliance:

- I am too tired to try.
- I just don't care anymore.
- It's not worth the effort.
- I don't have what it takes.
- I'm not prepared or organized enough.
- I'm not ready.

> *"There are countless ways of attaining greatness. But any road to reaching one's maximum potential must be built on a bedrock of respect for the individual, a commitment to excellence, and a rejection of mediocrity."*
>
> *Buck Rodgers, IBM*

The key to moving away from the mundane is to actively reject these beliefs and replace them with the six tools necessary for excellence:

1. Energy
2. Passion
3. Pro-activity

4. Preparation and Support
5. Focus
6. Direction

1. Energy for Excellence

To rebuild a belief and expand your excellence, you need physical energy. Plenty of rest, healthy nutrition, and physical fitness will enhance any project you take on as you feed and care for your brain. In 2009, the Centers for Disease Control declared insufficient sleep as a public health epidemic. In their survey, over 30% of adults reported getting less than 6 hours sleep per night. Too often individuals boast about their lack of need for sleep, but studies show that while we may get used to sleeping less and less, our brains suffer for it. Insufficient sleep has been connected to disease, weight gain, accidents, and poor performance on tests.[1] Our brains require rest to provide the amount of focus and perseverance necessary to succeed. Our brains also need healthy food and exercise. In his book *Making a Good Brain Great*, clinical neuroscientist and brain imaging expert Dr. Daniel Amen suggests seven steps to promote brain health:

1. Increase water intake. Dr. Amen suggests at least 84 ounces per day.
2. Reduce the number of calories you consume and make those calories count.
3. Increase the amount of omega-3 fatty acids in your diet. Most of the brain is made up of DHA, one form of omega-3 fatty acid, so replenish its supply.
4. Increase your intake of antioxidants from fruits and vegetables to prevent deterioration and early aging in your brain.
5. Enjoy a diet with a good balance of proteins, healthy fats and carbohydrates. Avoid diets that eliminate one specific food group—your body needs balance.
6. Eat super foods (e.g. blueberries, peppers, and broccoli) that are high in color and rich in vitamins and minerals.
7. Plan your snacks and make healthy choices.[2]

Physical exercise is an essential component for creating mental energy. Studies show that people who exercise regularly sleep better, maintain a healthy weight, and experience more mental alertness and a sense of emotional well-being. Thirty minutes a day of exercise has been shown to offer each of these benefits.

As you pursue excellence, pursue good health. Know your numbers (e.g., blood pressure, iron, and thyroid) and work to get them in an optimal range. A healthy body will give you the edge and the confidence you need to believe in your excellence.

2. Passion for the Process

Once your body is fueled, you must fuel your mind and soul with passion. Mediocrity will slip in when you lack passion for your work and your projects. Chapter 9 will discuss finding your passions in more depth. You can motivate yourself to complete more mundane tasks by linking them to things you are passionate about. You might not be all that excited about completing paperwork, but by focusing on the end result and visualizing the payoff once it is finished, your passion will energize your efforts.

Tapping into your deepest desires and linking them to your project will enable you to overcome challenges along the way.

3. Increasing Initiative

Once your body and soul are ready to take on a task, it is time to get to it. Taking immediate action, even the smallest step, is essential to avoiding procrastination. Initiative is so important that an entire chapter has been devoted to it. Chapter 5 is about shifting your beliefs around your ability to take meaningful action toward your goals.

4. Preparation and Support

Preparation is a key component to excellence, as is finding the right team to support your efforts. Begin with mental preparation. Rehearse what it is you are seeking to accomplish and visualize each step. Research shows that this type of rehearsal activates your brain just as if you were actually completing the task. Once you have mentally rehearsed, you will have a better idea of what resources you will need to gather, including support. Identify what parts of a project you need to complete yourself, and then delegate the rest to competent team members. If you don't have a team, create one! All too often individuals avoid creating a team or hiring support staff because they believe that it will take more time to find and train the right people than to do it themselves. This is poor planning and very poor management. Your excellence will not be able to shine if your time is taken up completing tasks that do not highlight your strengths. Delegation is a major component of creating success.

5. Two Types of Focus

Focused attention has been the subject of years of research completed by Dr. Robert Nideffer. He describes two types of processes: automatic and controlled (or conscious) attention. Automatic attention is what occurs when an experienced driver drives along a familiar route. When you drive home from work, you are able to listen to music, carry on a conversation, and enjoy the scenery without conscious thought about how far to turn the steering wheel or press on the brake. This automatic attention is what athletes and artists experience when they are "in the zone". Being in the zone is exactly where you want to be to create excellence.

There is no shortcut to get into the zone. This ability only comes with practice. When a task is new, controlled or conscious attention is required. This is a different, more laborious type of focus. The more time you put into developing a skill, the more automatic it becomes. Practice also creates confidence.

Like driving, eating is an automatic process. You hold your food and bring it to your mouth without effort and usually without error. Dr. Nideffer uses eating to demonstrate how attention and confidence are important to the performance of a task. He also uses an exercise to show how automatic focus can be broken down by a lack of confidence. In this exercise subjects are told to take a match and bring it up like a piece of food and then put it in their mouth. If the subject is able to close his mouth tightly, the match will go out because of a lack of oxygen. If he fails to close his mouth, he gets burned.[3] I do NOT suggest you try this, but imagine the difficulty you would have extinguishing a match in your mouth. The automatic focus would be broken.

What was an automatic process has become a very conscious one. Fear of getting burned and a lack of trust that the match will go out has damaged your confidence and your focus. If your confidence is low, the heat you feel from the match will create more doubt and your mouth will tense up, making it difficult to close your lips. Failing to close your lips will result in your getting burned. Getting burned by this exercise will reduce your confidence even more as your fear and lack of trust increase. The chances of ever successfully closing your mouth around a burning match are very slim.

What does this exercise have to do with excellence? Whenever you try something new, your confidence is lower than when you do something familiar. Failure takes your confidence even lower. Practice is the only thing that will create the type of focus that is automatic and confident. Practice also builds trust and eliminates fear as the new skill becomes more and more familiar. In order to get "in the zone" you must lose your fear, create trust and confidence, and complete tasks automatically rather than consciously. This is the key to effortless success.

6. A Sense of Direction

When I moved from the West Coast to the Midwest, it took me a long time to regain a sense of direction. Navigating around the San Francisco Bay Area was simple for me as long as I knew where the ocean was. But there was no ocean as a reference point for me in Iowa. Or mountains for that matter! I had to find new reference points.

A sense of direction is vital to creating excellence. Like a trip in your car, your process will have a starting place, reference points along the way, and a specific destination. Excellence is dependent upon reference points or markers that let you know you are on the right path. Clarity on where you are going and how you are going to get there is essential.

Believing that you can navigate from point A to point B is necessary if you are ever going to arrive. This clarity will come from a strong sense of purpose (discussed in Chapter 9).

Each of these tools represents a moment by moment choice. These are the tools that begin to shift your belief from mediocrity toward excellence.

A great deal of research has been done in the area of peak or optimal performance in sports psychology that can be applied to life in general. Optimal performance, like excellence, is an extraordinary experience. Athletes, performers, and artists describe total focus, extreme confidence, and a total loss of self-consciousness. Some say that they lose all sense of time or as if things are moving in slow motion. This is more than being "in the zone". An individual in this state has begun to experience "flow". When you experience flow, you are completed absorbed in the experience, and it is effortless and pleasurable.[4] When you experience both being in the zone and flow, you will find yourself performing at a level higher than you ever expected. Your skills improve as you feel unrushed and at ease. Distractions are not a threat to your performance, because your confidence allows you to focus on those reference points described above and refocus quickly when necessary. Your preparation and practice pays off. Excellence flows.

Perfectionism

In researching *Your Belief Quotient* it was surprising to discover the high number of people who believe they strive for excellence but how few of these people believe they ever achieve it. Digging deeper we found skewed perceptions about mediocrity, excellence and perfectionism. Many of those we interviewed believed that if they were not the best in their field, they were not excellent and therefore were mediocre. This definition of excellence is based on comparing yourself and your work to others. The weakness in this method of defining excellence is that the measure is a moveable object and very subjective. Excellence needs to be based on an objective measure, goal or target.

During our interviews, we also talked to a number of people who believed that excellence means perfection. These folks analyze their efforts and scrutinize for any possible flaw. Praise for their work is discounted because they can always find something that could be better. They cannot ever claim excellence because perfection is an impossible goal.

Perfectionism is not what most of us think it is. The word "perfection" is from the Latin "perfectio," and "perfect" comes from the Latin word "perfectus." These expressions come from "perficio"—"to finish", "to bring to an end." "Perfectio(n)" actually means "a finishing", and "perfect(us)" means "finished".[5] All of us who obsessively pick at a project hoping to perfect it are truly delaying the perfection, the finishing, of whatever it is we are working on.

> *"Perfectionism is the voice of the oppressor, the enemy of the people. It will keep you cramped and insane your whole life . . . I think perfectionism is based on the obsessive belief that if you run carefully enough, hitting each stepping-stone just right, you won't have to die. The truth is that you will die anyway and that a lot of people who aren't even looking at their feet are going to do a whole lot better than you, and have a lot more fun while they're doing it."*
>
> *Anne Lamott*

Marcy's Battle with Perfectionism

Marcy was proud to call herself a perfectionist. She believed her perfectionism drove her work, kept her standards high, and made her products among the best in the market. Marcy designed and created beautiful high end garments with a creative artistic flair. Her work was in high demand for women who attend elegant events, and they were willing to pay a premium price for Marcy's creations. Marcy's business had plateaued, and she was beginning to worry about making enough profit to cover her costs when she contacted us for business coaching. Marcy's primary concern was cash flow. She was fearful about how the economy was affecting her business. She was worried about attracting new customers and charging enough to cover her costs and make a profit.

After we interviewed Marcy about her operations we came to a different conclusion. We knew **Marcy would not be able to continue to grow if she didn't break through one specific belief barrier: her belief that her products had to be perfect before they could be released.**

Marcy would work for hours and hours getting designs to work, seams to match, and fabrics to lay just right. Every stitch was scrutinized and if it wasn't perfect, it was torn out and done over. Perfectionism took a terrible physical and mental toll on Marcy, but it was also destroying her relationships with customers and employees. Marcy's customers were often disappointed when deadlines were pushed forward again and again. Marcy wasn't willing to let them have anything but her very best work. One custom wedding gown took twice as long as expected, and Marcy was still fussing over details just hours before the bride was due to walk down the aisle. Marcy had a hard time finding employees to help her on the crafting of her garments, because no one's skills were ever good enough. She was never harsh in her criticism, but she frequently would go back behind the scenes and redo sections completed by an employee. This made her staff feel embarrassed and frustrated. Marcy's near obsession with perfection kept her from spending adequate time running her business and taking care of marketing and accounting. If Marcy didn't change the way she did business, she wouldn't have a business much longer.

Marcy's perfectionism looked very different at home. Marcy spent so many hours in her studio, that when she got home she had little time for cleaning and organizing. Counters, closets, and cupboards were stacked and stuffed full of haphazard piles and no one knew where to find anything. Marcy's thinking was if she couldn't take the time to do it right, she wouldn't even start to put things in order. She rarely asked her children to help her clean; she knew she would end up doing it over. Marcy was modeling some very destructive behavior for her children. One daughter was becoming just as perfectionistic as Marcy, nagging the other children to pick up after themselves and obsessing about keeping her own room spotless. Marcy's son wasn't learning how to organize his belongings, and he frequently lost school assignments and parts of his sports uniform. The chaos at home was one of the driving factors that led Marcy to move her business to a studio. She couldn't work in the middle of all the clutter and didn't want customers to see how she lived. Shame was eating away at Marcy's soul.

Marcy saw her work as an extension of herself, but was in denial about how her home reflected her inner turmoil. Marcy was not a perfectionist. She was an "imperfectionist." She was constantly looking for the imperfections in her work, her employees, her home, and herself. Marcy saw perfection as the road to excellence. When she began to work on rebuilding the following five beliefs about excellence, she began to break free and function better at work and at home.

> *"At its root, perfectionism isn't really about a deep love of being meticulous. It's about fear. Fear of making a mistake. Fear of disappointing others. Fear of failure. Fear of success."*
>
> *Michael Law*

Excellence

Instead of pursuing perfectionism, expand into excellence. Embrace the five statements below and create better beliefs around your excellence.

1. **Excellence is a process, not an outcome.**
   Excellence is based on realistic, clearly defined goals, not on unreasonable aspirations. When pursuing excellence, we recognize that it is a journey and not just a destination. Focusing on the process of becoming excellent will yield better results because it allows for course corrections and new information.

   Better belief: "I am moving toward excellence every day."

2. **Excellence is a reflection of character, not achievement.**
   Instead of being driven by an unhealthy need to achieve

perfection, excellence comes from a healthy sense of self confidence. Excellence brings a sense of personal satisfaction and is not dependent on external recognition. Perfectionism is ego driven, always needing to be fed. Excellence is founded on a grounded sense of self.

Better belief: "I am confident in my ability to be excellent in all I do."

3. **Excellence allows for learning from mistakes, not harsh criticism**. Excellence is willing to risk failure and does not avoid situations that may expose a lack of mastery. Perfectionism is haunted by the voice of the relentless inner critic. Excellence has learned to silence the inner critic and make an objective examination of progress and results.

   Better belief: "I am learning and growing in joy."

4. **Excellence sees others in a supportive role, not an adversarial role**. Perfectionism constantly compares and almost always comes up short in the comparison. Excellence enjoys healthy competition, and is unthreatened by others.

   Better belief: "I am working and collaborating with others who support my pursuit of excellence."

5. **Excellence is willing to wait for mastery to be achieved and does not expect immediate results.** Excellence is not demanding, but allowing. Excellence adds peace and joy, not frustration or anger. Excellence focuses on a specific area of mastery and accepts that there are areas where excellence should not be a focus because of a lack of aptitude or interest.

   Better belief: "I am getting better every day at the things I am working on."

Personal Standards of Excellence

Whether you are mired in mediocrity or making yourself crazy with perfectionism, there are three important steps to moving toward excellence:

First, embrace the discomfort that comes from change and growth. Mediocrity recoils from this type of change as it threatens its existence. The moment you begin moving forward, you are less and less mediocre. Perfectionism resists growth, as ego insists that it is perfect and doesn't need to change. Once the perfectionist accepts that their beliefs are not helping them achieve their goal, excellence will begin to emerge.

Second, get clear on what exactly it is you want. What are the passions driving you toward your goal and how will you know it when you get there? Getting clear on your objective will keep you from drifting into mediocrity or distracting yourself with perfectionism.

Finally, raise your standards. This may sound unnecessary to the perfectionist, but keep Mary's struggles at home in mind as you consider the need for high standards. Many perfectionists settle and tolerate things like poor organization in their home because they are choosing to focus on just one area. They will even resort to hiding the truth of messy closets or unbalanced checkbooks out of shame.

Both ends of the spectrum, those struggling with mediocrity and with perfectionism, will benefit from creating high personal standards. At the end of this chapter is a checklist of areas to consider raising your personal standards**. When you set high personal standards and maintain them, you create a stronger sense of well-being and confidence.** You will find yourself strengthening your relationships with others and attracting people with the same standards and goals. Your standards communicate your beliefs around excellence. Review the checklist of standards below and create an action plan of how you will become excellent in each one. Creating excellence in one area of your life will allow you to believe in and create excellence in the rest of your life.

EXERCISES for Expanding Excellence:

1. Affirmations for Excellence

Write affirmations about your deepest desires for excellence. Ask yourself:

- What thinking patterns or beliefs would I like to change?
- What circumstances would I like to improve or transform?
- What experiences would I like to have?
- What feelings would I like to enjoy?
- What do I want my life to be like?

You can write as many or as few affirmations as you like. You might make a list of several based on the examples in this chapter and rotate through them over the course of a week or month. Take time to read through each of your affirmations, letting the words and ideas sink in before moving on to the next.

2. Eliminate Mediocrity

Raise your standards in the areas of your life where you have been tolerating mediocrity. Complete the checklist below (adapted from a list created by the 'Father of Coaching' Thomas Leonard)[6], create an action plan for the one item that bothers you the most. Check back at the end of each week to measure your progress. Do this each week for 10 weeks (90 days) and you will have formed new habits of excellence in your life and better beliefs about what you can accomplish. Work your way through the list to create high personal standards in every area of your life.

Rate yourself on the following:

Item	Excellent	OK	Needs Improved
The way I dress & keep my clothing.			
The way I speak. (the language I use)			
The way I keep my car.			
The way I treat people.			
The way I take care of my body.			
The way I show gratitude.			
The way I keep my work organized.			
The way I keep my home.			
The way I handle money.			
The way I spend my time.			

What I will do specifically to create change in the areas that need improvement:

____

____

____

____

3. Track Your Progress

Since excellence is a process, not a destination, choose a specific task or project and track your progress toward excellence. Find ways to become objective in assessing and measuring your skill or work. For example, if you want to be an excellent salesman, track your progress on how many sales calls you initiate each week. You cannot control the variables on how many sales you actually get, but you can measure your efforts in making contacts with potential customers. If you want to be an excellent parent, track your progress on how consistently you reinforce your child's good behavior. Choose an area, set a specific target behavior, and track your progress.

4. Limit Your Time to Scrutinize

Set time limits on projects when you find yourself over-analyzing or scrutinizing your work. A client told me it would usually take her 5 hours to write a 500-word article for a newsletter. I suggested she give herself a time limit of one hour, leave the article until the end of business, and then read it once more before sending it out. She tried this and found the time limit pushed her to get it done and to stop analyzing every word.

5. Chunk It

Break large projects into smaller, more manageable chunks. It is difficult to believe in excellence when you are tired or overwhelmed. Working on smaller pieces of a project will allow you to keep your energy and passion for the work high.

6. Invite Constructive Criticism

When you believe in your excellence you will be confident enough to ask for and receive useful feedback. Establish parameters for the critique. Choose your critic wisely and tell them exactly what type of feedback you want. Do you want help changing something, input on resources, or just a reaction of whether something is good or bad? You decide what type of criticism you are open to receiving.

7. Find an Accountability Partner

Excellent people connect with one another in productive and meaningful ways. An accountability partner can challenge and encourage you. Your accountability partner needs to be objective, so he/she should probably not be a family member or spouse. Set regular times to connect and develop transparency and trust.

8. Work with a Mentor or Coach

Olympic athletes never attempt to compete without the guidance and support of a coach. Neither should you. Your coach should be experienced and able to give you objective feedback, suggestions for improvement, and inspire you to go further than you ever have before. A mentor is usually someone experienced in your field that is willing to share their expertise. A trainer is skilled at imparting knowledge you need to succeed. A coach has been trained to pull ideas and actions out of you that you didn't know were there. Determine which of these you need and develop a relationship with them.

9. Peak Performance

Get a health physical and determine whether your body is fit enough to support your pursuit of excellence. Consider working with a naturopathic physician to measure your levels of vitamins, thyroid, hormones, etc. If your health is mediocre, chances are your performance will be too.

CHAPTER 7

ACCEPTING ABUNDANCE

[*uh*-**buhn**-d*uh*ns] A great or plentiful amount;
fullness to overflowing.

"Whatever we are waiting for—peace of mind, contentment, grace, the inner awareness of simple abundance—it will surely come to us, but only when we are ready to receive it with an open and grateful heart."
Sarah Ban Breathnach

ABUNDANCE

ENTITLEMENT SCARCITY

Abundance is the belief that there is more than enough. In an abundant universe, you have plenty of time, money, health, energy and wisdom. Abundance is the knowledge that you can give it all away and there will still be enough for yourself. Abundance expands with heartfelt gratitude and humility. At its core, an abundance mentality springs from a healthy sense of personal worth and builds on one's personal and spiritual values. Dr. Stephen Covey coined the phrase "abundance mindset" in his best-seller *The Seven Habits of Highly Effective People*. According to Covey, an abundance mentality is "a paradigm that there is plenty out there and enough to spare for everybody."[1]

Nature gives us wonderful examples of abundance, particularly in the growth cycle of trees and flowers. After a period of dormancy, a fruit tree bursts into blooms and is covered in an abundance of flowers. Wind and rain might buffet the tree and destroy many of the flowers. An average of 75% of the flowers will fall, but those buds remaining will eventually grow into fruit. A fruit tree is not designed to have every flower pollinate and grow into fruit. The tree does not have the resources to sustain every flower. The larger and stronger the tree's branches and internal supports, the greater the capacity it will have to bear more fruit.[2] Once the tree bears fruit, every piece of fruit contains seeds, and every seed contains an incalculable number of trees and fruit. This is abundance!

This illustration fits the human experience of abundance well. We also go through periods of dormancy. These periods are times of quiet growth and strengthening. During dormancy, a fruit tree rests and its sap slows. It is the perfect time to prune away dead branches and treat any disease. As humans, we need time to pull back and reflect on what needs pruned away. We need time to heal and refresh. The end of dormancy comes after the tree has been exposed to chilling temperatures and the weather begins to warm. People awaken and grow as they warm up to new ideas and opportunities. Tree growth during the spring is dependent upon the quality and quantity of sunlight, water, and soil. Our growth as individuals is equally dependent on how we feed ourselves: body, mind and spirit. Abundance requires preparation. Once those flowers begin to emerge from the branches, only the most resilient survive to become fruit. The initial beauty of the petals fall away as the fruit emerges and ripens. The intoxicating sweetness of fully matured fruit arrives after being warmed by the summer sunlight. Wind, rain, and heat are metaphors for the challenges we must face to grow and be prepared for abundance. Once we begin to bear fruit in our lives, we witness firsthand the ever expanding cycle of abundance.

I go into the detail of the growth cycle of fruit trees for a purpose: Abundance does not magically appear. There are myths circulating that we can engage in wishful thinking and expect abundance to appear. This is simply not true. That is not to say that abundance, when it occurs is not surprising. Manifesting abundance can seem magical, but it is always the result of a cycle of preparation. It is my intention to help you understand how to be ready to receive abundance in your life. Your beliefs about abundance are crucial to your success in life and business.

A Scarcity Mentality

> *"People with a scarcity mentality tend to see everything in terms of win-lose. There is only so much; and if someone else has it, that means there will be less for me. The more principle-centered we become, the more we develop an abundance mentality, and the more we are genuinely happy for the successes, well-being, achievements, recognition, and good fortune of other people. We believe their success adds to . . . rather than detracts from . . . our lives."*
>
> *Stephen Covey*

The Belief Quotient assessment measured your beliefs about abundance versus scarcity and entitlement. At one end of the abundance continuum is scarcity, the belief that there is not enough. A scarcity mentality becomes grasping and tight-fisted because it is based on fear. There is a constant wariness and watchfulness that shows up with scarcity. Every penny, every moment, every crumb must be monitored, hoarded, and protected.

Many of us were raised with varying degrees of a scarcity mentality. It is this mentality that creates the belief that money is somehow evil or bad. We have decades of cultural icons that demonstrate this belief. In movies like 'It's a Wonderful Life,' the bad guy is rich. On television, if someone has a big house or fancy car, they are suspected of foul play. As a young teen I was encouraged to read a series of novels that seemed to follow a formula: a poor, sweet, clean-faced girl falls in love with the boy interested in the short-haired rich girl who wears red lipstick and spends way too much of her daddy's money on clothes. The rich girl always ended up miserable and alone. The message I got was that wealthy people lack character and have materialistic values. No wonder so many ministers, conscious business owners, and spiritual entrepreneurs struggle financially. If we believe wealth is evil, we will unconsciously sabotage any effort to attract financial success.

No doubt you've heard the expression that money is the root of all evil, but that isn't an accurate quotation. The actual quotation says:

> *"For the love of money is a root of all kinds of evil. Some people, eager for money, have wandered from the faith and pierced themselves with many griefs."*
>
> *I Timothy 6:10* [3]

"The love of money" is the root of evil. Making money the central focus of your life will lead to all kinds of problems. But having and enjoying money is not wrong or any indication of poor values. A scarcity mentality makes possessing money and other resources the focus, where abundance recognizes and receives the flow of resources in our lives.

A scarcity mentality has also been called a competitive mindset. The competitive mindset believes that there can only be one winner, that there is only so much achievement, glory, success or wealth to go around. People with this mentality are "always comparing, always competing," says Stephen Covey.[4] This view looks at the world as if there is just one piece of pie left and everyone wants it. To achieve my goals with this mindset, I have to beat my competitors to the customers, the cash, the book contract, the sale, the products; you fill in the blank with whatever it is you know you compete for in the marketplace. Jealousy results when someone else gets what you aspired to have. Negative emotions drive wedges between people. A scarcity mentality can eat away at the soul of a company when coworkers compete for the same job. The same applies when two businesses try to offer the same product or service to the same customer. People with a scarcity mentality have difficulty celebrating the successes of others because of the belief that it somehow takes something away from them. They might say "congratulations" with a smile on their face, but inside it is eating their hearts out.

An abundant mindset eliminates a competitive spirit and invites collaboration. I learned this when I joined a local group of professional life and business coaches. I had recently left a corporate job and was fairly new to coaching at the time. I was impressed with how the men and women in this group encouraged and supported one another. The group embraced several core values including "We live in an Abundant Universe." The leader of the group demonstrated that belief when she told me how pleased she was that one of her clients had stopped working with her and had begun working with me. She genuinely felt that the client would benefit from the change. She could respond this way because she was confident that her practice would always be full with ideal clients. She practiced an abundance mentality in every aspect of her work. Without an abundance mentality, this could have been a very awkward situation, but this coach and I went on to collaborate on projects in the group and developed a strong respect for one another.

In another example, I had two clients who each owned auto repair shops within ten miles of each other. Joe and John had met at a business seminar and decided to hold each another accountable for putting what they had learned into practice. These two men got together every week for lunch to talk about how they were managing and marketing their businesses. When Joe started working with me and seeing improvement in his life and business, he urged John to call me and work with me as well. When John's shop began offering tires for sale in addition to auto repair, Joe's shop sent customers there to buy tires. When Joe hired a technician with specialty skills, John sent customers needing those services to Joe's shop. Both men were confident in their skills as businessmen and in the value offered in their shops. This collaborative friendship was a source of encouragement and support that both men felt contributed to their success as business owners. A scarcity mentality or competitive mindset would have kept these businessmen from the success they realized through collaboration.

> *"Abundance Mentality means that rather than seeing life as a competition with only one winner, you see it as a cornucopia of ever enlarging opportunity, resources and wealth. You don't compare yourself to others and are genuinely happy*

> *for their successes . . . Those with the Abundance Mentality see their competitors as some of their most valued and important teachers."*
>
> *Stephen Covey*

Eaten Away by Entitlement

At the other end of the spectrum from scarcity you will find entitlement. A sense of entitlement is the belief that life's blessings are owed to you. Like an abundance mentality, there is an assumption that good things are coming but these gifts are received without grace or gratitude. There is the same grasping and selfishness seen with a scarcity mentality. With both scarcity and entitlement there is never enough. Themes of gratitude, generosity and humility dry up when your belief system is out of balance. People with personality disorders frequently have a sense of entitlement as they place an elevated sense of importance to their own emotional needs. In the case of a personality disorder, there is no sense of shame or embarrassment in demanding to have needs and wants met. There is no sense of reality when they expect to be treated like rock stars or royalty. Don't assume that if you fail to demand diva status that you are free from a sense of entitlement. This faulty belief can creep up and overtake you if you are not careful. Employees frequently fall into an entitlement mentality, expecting to use sick days for time off, taking advantage of company perks like free soda or coffee, and expecting salary increases every year. When did "bonus pay" become an expectation? There is a danger of coming to expect privileges as always available and taking an employer's graciousness for granted. This is how entitlement can creep up on you. We get used to enjoying certain privileges and come to expect them to always be there.

When we have an abundance mentality, we take notice of blessings as they come our way and humbly express gratitude. Overcoming an entitlement mindset is not easy. We often do not even realize we are expecting more than we are due. But those living with an attitude of entitlement miss out on the flow of abundance. You cannot demand that a river flow in a certain direction. You can guide it and make way for it, but simply expecting the water to flow toward you is unreasonable. If you realize that you are missing out on the generous flow of money, time, health or other resources, check to see if there is some area of your life where you are failing to practice gratitude. Ask trusted friends or mentors if they see an entitlement attitude in you and be open to their response. When you become aware of this attitude, eliminate it with a mindfulness practice. Being mindful of the smallest gifts and expressing gratitude for them will radically alter your outlook. A number of gratitude exercises are outlined at the end of this chapter that will help you.

Spirituality and Abundance

Abundance is a spiritual concept. You can see the evidence of abundance in a life of prosperity and freedom from want. You cannot see abundance at work. The process of abundance works its way into the material world through the spirit, mind and emotions. Your strengths, gifts, talents, education, experience or profession may be the instrument of prosperity, but God is the Ultimate Source. The infinite supply of abundance is channeled through the character of God Himself and communicated to us by grace. Regardless of your spiritual beliefs, this gracious gift of abundance is available to you. Just as the rain falls on all of us, abundance is accessible to everyone.

God is love, and He expresses His love toward us by meeting our every need in His perfect timing. Every need has been anticipated and the fulfillment of that need is readily available when we are ready to receive it. Jesus said,

> *"Therefore I tell you, do not worry about your life, what you will eat or drink; or about your body, what you will wear. Is not life more than food, and the body more than clothes? Look at the birds of the air; they do not sow or reap or store away in barns, and yet your heavenly Father feeds them. Are*

> *you not much more valuable than they?* [27] *Can any one of you by worrying add a single hour to your life?*
>
> *"And why do you worry about clothes? See how the flowers of the field grow. They do not labor or spin. Yet I tell you that not even Solomon in all his splendor was dressed like one of these. If that is how God clothes the grass of the field, which is here today and tomorrow is thrown into the fire, will he not much more clothe you—you of little faith? So do not worry, saying, 'What shall we eat?' or 'What shall we drink?' or 'What shall we wear?' For the pagans run after all these things, and your heavenly Father knows that you need them. But seek first his kingdom and his righteousness, and all these things will be given to you as well. Therefore do not worry about tomorrow, for tomorrow will worry about itself. Each day has enough trouble of its own." Matthew 6:25-34* [7]

"Are you not much more valuable than they (the birds)?" We are reminded here that abundance hinges on the exceptional value God has placed on every man and woman. We do not receive abundance based on any effort or merit of our own, but because of grace. We can't increase abundance in our lives through sheer effort or worry. The one thing we must do to experience abundance is to focus on the Divine purpose for which we were created. Part of that purpose is to live free from the lies and self-sabotaging beliefs that keep us from experiencing all the abundance available to us.

Abundance and prosperity is generally associated with financial wealth, but it is so much more. Abundance is not just about money. There is an abundance of time, health, influence, support, and any other resource you can imagine you would ever want or need. The imagination is a wonderful tool when it comes to an abundance mentality.

> *"Now to Him Who, by the action of His power that is at work within us, is able to carry out His purpose and do superabundantly, far over and above all that we dare ask or*

think infinitely beyond our highest prayers, desires, thoughts, hopes, or dreams." Ephesians 6:20

I get excited every time I read or think of that verse. We are Divinely empowered to fulfill the purpose for which we were designed and have every resource we could possibly imagine at our disposal. That is abundance! Our challenge is to be ready to recognize and receive those resources. Recognizing those resources requires that we open our minds to realities beyond our physical senses and live by the principles that create that abundance.

Seven Universal Laws of Abundance

Principles or Universal Laws always work, whether you believe or understand them or not. Brian Tracy compares Universal Laws to telephone numbers. Dial a phone number and you will be connected to the phone associated with that number regardless of your education, intellect, mindset, or spirituality. Dial incorrectly, and you will not get the result you wanted.[9] Universal Laws are dependable, practical, and inviolable. Just as in mathematics 1 + 1 always equals 2, Universal Laws always add up to results of blessings and abundance. The more you study and apply these truths to your daily living, the more results you will see.

The Universal Law of Vacuum

"Clutter is stuck energy. The word 'clutter' derives from the Middle English word 'clotter' which means to coagulate—and that's about as stuck as you can get."

Karen Kingston

One way to bring more abundance into your life is to create more space. You have heard the phrase, "Nature abhors a vacuum." **When you eliminate clutter and clear space in your life, you will find**

abundance moving in to fill the space. If you want more time and clearer thought in your work, de-clutter your office. This is something I encourage all my clients to do. It is surprising how much easier it is to work in an organized space. Piles of papers and books are distracting and can leach away energy. If you want newer, better clothing, clean out your closets and drawers. I have discovered that when I release items I don't use or wear any more that I often will find just the garment I've been wanting on sale. Abundance is much like a river or stream. It needs to flow. When water pools off to the side of a stream, it becomes stagnant. If you find things getting dull, clear space and allow abundance to flow.

If it is impossible to actually create the vacuum, you can use mental imagery to put this law to work. You will remember how I explained that your brain perceives visualization and rehearsal in the same way as actual activity. In her book, *The Dynamic Laws of Prosperity*, Catherine Ponder describes how a man visualized the rooms of his house as empty as the result of it being sold. He pictured his house being emptied room by room by the movers he planned to hire. He had been trying to sell his house for months without success, but this exercise of mentally creating a vacuum worked. Within days of doing the exercise a buyer appeared and paid full price for the man's home.

A client of mine named Shelly used this type of mental imagery to replace her car. Her old car was beyond repair and barely got her to work without overheating. As a single mom, Shelly didn't have very much set aside for a new car. She needed the car to get around, so she couldn't get rid of it to create space, but felt she needed to create a vacuum to attract a newer car. After a brainstorming session, she decided to try clearing space in her garage. There was room for her car, but the rest of the space was filled with items that needed recycled or taken to the dump. She spent a weekend clearing out her garage and felt great about the space she had opened. On Monday morning, Shelly chugged into the parking lot at work and was embarrassed when a co-worker noticed the steam coming from under the hood. He came over to see if he could help and Shelly told him she was looking for a newer car. The co-worker excitedly told her about a ministry at his church where they gave restored cars to single moms. Shelly called the ministry team that day, and within a week had a much newer, nicer car.

Service providers are often stuck in a scarcity mentality when it comes to attracting clients. All too often they accept anyone willing to pay for their services, whether or not they are ideal clients. Jane was struggling with this issue in her coaching practice. When we began working together, Jane clearly defined her ideal client and what she had to offer. When I asked her about the clients she was seeing, Jane admitted that two of them were not ideal clients. One client lacked commitment. He griped about the cost of coaching, showed up late for appointments, and often failed to do his homework. Another client wanted to work on issues that did not fit Jane's expertise. Jane came to me because she wanted her practice to grow, so she wasn't thrilled when I suggested she let these two clients go. After giving it some thought, Jane decided to let the first client go. The next week Jane was excited. She realized that she had been carrying resentment and frustration toward this client and it was a relief to not have to deal with him anymore. She felt energized and happier in her work. That happiness dimmed a bit when I suggested she follow through and let the second client go. This client was a joy to work with and gladly paid for her sessions, but her goals had shifted. Jane recognized that referring her client to someone with a niche that matched the client would be right thing to do. Jane called me a few days later and shared that she had talked with her client. The client was so impressed with Jane's integrity and appreciated the referral to a new coach so much, that she has become a raving fan. A raving fan is a customer who sends friends and family to you for business out of appreciation and gratitude. Jane's raving fan referred four new clients in the next three months. Jane experienced abundance because she created a vacuum and stayed true to her integrity.

Another area where the Universal Law of Vacuum works is in our relationships. Kathy wanted desperately to be married again. She was divorced a number of years ago when her husband left her for another woman. Kathy came to me to work on self-limiting beliefs around her work, but during our conversations, her feelings toward her ex-husband would come up. She thought about him every day. She wondered about what life would have been if they had not divorced. She yearned for the home they shared. She was stuck in the past. I asked for permission to ask a few questions about this area of Kathy's life. Those questions helped Kathy recognize that she could not attract a new man into her life while she was still focused on her ex-husband. Kathy needed to release the connection she had to her ex-husband. By forgiving her ex-husband for his affair, she cut the emotional ties that held her in a relationship that didn't exist anymore. Kathy let go of the past and began to prepare for a new relationship. Forgiveness is how we clear space and make room emotionally for better relationships. When we hang on to hurt or resentment, we are emotionally tied to the past and are unable to move forward in a current relationship or a new one. Releasing negative emotions like anger, bitterness and resentment cuts ties to old patterns and creates the free flow of abundance.

Where do you need to create space or vacuum in your life? Do you have piles of stuff leaching energy and dragging you down? Are you hanging on to objects or people with a sense of fear that they cannot be replaced? Do you need to mentally create space in some area of your physical, mental, or spiritual environment? Put the Universal Law of Vacuum to work and see how abundance flows in to fill the space.

The Universal Law of Affirmation

"High expectations are the key to everything."
Sam Walton

The Law of Affirmation is the principle by which you declare what it is you are claiming through abundance. This law includes the Law of Belief and the Law of Expectation. These laws state that **whatever you truly believe or expect becomes your reality**. This belief incorporates your mind, will and emotions. To put the Law of Affirmation to work, you must know and believe with all the force of your will and emotions. When you expect good things to happen, they generally do. When you expect negative things to happen, you usually end up patting yourself on the back for being right. People and circumstances reflect your attitudes back at you like a mirror.

I learned the power of this law when I first started teaching. I read about research that revealed how students tend to live up to their teachers' expectations.[11] In this study, one group of teachers were told that their students were exceptionally talented with above average intelligence. A second group of teachers were told that their students were poor achievers, had behavioral problems, and had lower than average intelligence. The truth was that both groups included a mix of excellent and poor students. At the end of the year, the teachers who expected poor performance found their students achieved average results. However, the teachers who expected excellence found that their students lived up to their expectations.

I decided to try a version of this study in my own classroom. I worked in a private school for children with learning and behavior disorders. My students had failed in regular education classrooms before coming to this school. They came with thick files including diagnostic tests and reports of behavioral problems. Instead of reading my students' files and learning about the challenges they had faced in school before coming to me, I decided to assume that every student was exceptionally gifted and well behaved. My mentor teacher thought this was an excellent idea, but several of my colleagues thought I was being naïve. Regardless of those opinions, I started the year out by sharing my expectation with my students and their parents that every one of my students would succeed. I believe the exceptional results my students showed at the end of the year had more to do with my expectations than with my skills as a teacher. Every student in that classroom made academic gains of at least 2 years or more in reading, mathematics, and science. That year was transformational for several of these students. One boy went from a first grade reading level to a fourth grade level. When he started the year he was being treated for anxiety and depression, largely due to his problems in school. Halfway into the school year, his mother came to me with tears of joy because her boy was back enjoying the things boys love, free of medication and the nightmares that had plagued him. This boy, who had been labeled a hopeless case, is now a medical doctor.

What happened in my classroom has happened for my clients' businesses, health and relationships. One of the things I do as a coach for my clients is believe in success for them until they believe it for themselves. I expect results from our work together and eventually, so do they. These results come from challenging self-limiting beliefs. Self-limiting beliefs are like an anchor lodged in scarcity and mediocrity. When you try to move forward, your limiting beliefs hold you back. Identifying the faulty belief, recognizing it as false, and then claiming the truth of abundance will help you achieve your dreams.

Always expect the best for yourself and the people around you. Don't be shy about telling people about what you expect to achieve. This is a great way to create accountability to pursue and achieve your goals.

The Universal Law of Attraction

> *"The successful warrior is the average man, with laser-like focus."*
>
> *Bruce Lee*

So much attention has been given to the Law of Attraction in recent years that I hesitate to include it here, but there are misconceptions to clarify and myths to expose. The Law of Attraction is one of the most powerful resources we have. When it is understood correctly and put to work, incredible things happen.

The Law of Attraction simply states that **you will attract the people, circumstances, and opportunities that are in line with your thoughts and desires**. This is not magic or some sort of New Age "woo-woo" nonsense. The Law of Attraction is a scientific fact: **what you put your attention on grows stronger**.

Putting the Law of Attraction to work is simply harnessing the power of your mind. In Chapter 2 you learned how your brain is designed to filter the millions of pieces of sensory data in your environment. The Reticular Activating System allows you to pay attention to only the few dozen items that are important to you at any given time. When you focus your attention on something, your brain searches incoming data for it, and makes it accessible to you by making you aware of its presence. It was there before you decided to focus on it; you just missed it as it flew by with a million other pieces of data. An example of this is when my husband bought his car. I didn't think I had ever seen the model he chose and thought the deep wine-red color was unique. I remember thinking, "This car will be easy to find in a parking lot." Was I wrong! A few weeks later I took his car to the shopping center and when I returned to the parking lot I found myself trying to open someone else's car. I looked around and saw there were at least four other cars the same color as my husband's, and one was the same make and model! I see cars similar to my husband's vehicle all the time now. That is because his car has special meaning for me. My brain looks for that car and separates out anything like it and sends that data to my mind.

This brain function is powerful when applied to attracting abundance into your life. When you determine to attract new business, you focus on your target market or your ideal customer. Soon you notice these potential customers everywhere. They begin to find you as well, because they have decided to seek out a business like yours. When you want a new relationship, and you have become clear on exactly the kind of person you are interested in meeting, that person shows up.

I know this works, because this is exactly how I found my husband. I had been divorced for a number of years and fully anticipated spending the rest of my life as a single woman. It wasn't until I went through *The Passion Test* [12] with another coach that I realized just how important being married was to me. I did not see myself as old and alone. *The Passion Test* helped me become clear on exactly what I wanted in a life partner. I was encouraged to list three to five "markers" or attributes that would confirm that I was living my passion. I started with five, and then wrote 25, and then I wrote 100 markers! I wanted to be completely clear on the kind of man I would be spending the rest of my life with. I love telling this story because it sounds so incredible. When I met the man who is now my husband and began to get to know him, I started ticking off things on my list. I was amazed to discover he had 99 out of 100 of the attributes on my list! The one thing my husband doesn't have is a good singing voice. (That's not unkind, just the simple truth!) When I made my list, I thought I wanted someone to sing with, but God in His infinite wisdom looked past what I wrote and gave me something better. What I really wanted was someone who loved music as much as I do. My husband has the largest and most eclectic music collection of anyone I know. The summer we dated, we went to hear 36 different rock bands, 5 plays and shows, and cranked up the tunes every time we hit the road. My dear husband is 100 out of 100. He is not perfect, but he is exactly the kind of man I wanted in my life.

My husband did not magically appear in my life one day. The Law of Attraction does not work based on wishful thinking. The Law of Attraction requires action. Once I knew I wanted to be married again and knew the kind of man I wanted to be married to, I needed to do my part. *The Passion Test* teaches a great system for taking action: Intention, Attention, No Tension. I set my intention when I described and visualized the man I wanted to marry. Next, I began to pay attention to everything I could possibly do to be ready for this man. Every time something showed up that would take me closer to making my vision real, I moved toward it. Chris and Janet Attwood say it this way:

> *"Every time you're faced with a choice, decision or opportunity, choose in favor of your passions."*

I had tried online dating years before all this and decided it wasn't for me. I met some wonderful men online, but the process was time consuming and rarely offered anyone in my local area that met my criteria. Just after I finished writing my markers for my intended husband, I received an e-mail from an online dating company I had once subscribed to. The e-mail caught my eye because the subject line talked about gratitude. I had the cursor of my mouse hovering over the delete button when the quote above popped into my mind. Here was an opportunity. Here was a chance to choose in favor of my passion for finding my husband. I was not excited about reopening my profile on this dating site, but I did it. The next day I hesitated before opening my e-mail. In the past I usually found seven or eight "matches" from the dating site. I dreaded wading through all those profiles to find "my guy." When I opened my e-mail, my heart sank with disappointment. There was only one e-mail from the dating site. I had set an intention that the process of meeting my husband would be easy. Having just one name in my inbox was certainly easy! When putting the Law of Attraction to work, once you've done everything you can, you relax and let the abundance flow. This is the next step: "No Tension".

I opened the e-mail and read the profile of the man I am now married to. I loved the photo he posted with his son. I valued his transparency about his life and was impressed with his personal goals. One word came to mind: "Possible." I thought, "It's possible this could be the guy." A year later we married, and after three years of sharing this story I still can't help but wonder over how amazing it is.

If you want abundance in your work, your health, your relationships—clearly define exactly what it is you want, put your attention on it, attach your emotions to it, take action, and then watch God work!

The Universal Law of Cause and Effect

The Law of Cause and Effect is based on the idea that everything happens for a reason. Since the days of Aristotle, countless philosophers and theologians have described the universe as having order, purpose and shape. This higher order dictates that every achievement, every success, every bit of abundance is the result of an action. If you believe the universe is random and that events are disconnected from purpose, you are more likely to struggle with the concept of abundance. Successfully attracting abundance or prosperity into your life is not a matter of luck. **Recognizing that you participate in the process of co-creating miracles through the actions you take creates a sense of empowerment and responsibility.**

This law has also been called the Law of Sowing and Reaping, the Law of Increase, and the Law of Expansion. In the Law of Sowing and Reaping, the type of results you yield is determined by the actions you take. Just as farmers harvest corn where they have planted corn, you reap what you have sown in your life. This is similar to the Buddhist concept of Karma, that your destiny is determined by your actions. In the Law of Sowing and Reaping, fate is not in control of your outcome, you are. Brian Tracy says *"It is not the world outside you that dictates your circumstances or conditions. It is the world inside you that creates the conditions of your life."*[13]

The story of the Sower has great application for us in business, relationships, and other areas of our lives. The Sower is an experienced farmer. He knows how to plant seed. The Sower has plenty of quality seed to plant. The method he uses in his time and culture is to toss seed out onto the ground. As the Sower tosses the seed, some falls by the wayside and birds come and eat it. The wise Sower ignores the birds and keeps sowing seeds. Another portion of seed falls on hard, rocky ground and is left exposed to the hot sun. This seed withers and dies. The Sower keeps sowing seed. Some of that seed falls among thorns and when the plants begin to grow, they are choked and die. The Sower keeps sowing seed. Some of that seed falls on good, fertile soil, takes root and grows. The Sower's persistence pays off and he reaps a bountiful harvest.[14]

Not every seed you sow will bear fruit. Some seed, or actions, will be stolen away. You might spend hours on a business proposal only to see the contract awarded to a competitor. Sometimes it will seem as though your efforts are withering and dying and failing to meet your expectations, like a new product line that never takes off. Other times it will seem as though forces beyond your control squeeze the life out of your business, like an economic downturn. But some seed will grow, and create an abundant harvest. When you keep sowing day after day into your business or your relationships, you will see progress.

If you are failing to reap the results you want in your life, it is necessary to examine the actions you took that created those results. What kind of seed are you sowing? This sounds simple, but this truth is often overlooked. It is a much harsher reality to take responsibility for every outcome in your life. It was hard for me to admit that my failed first marriage was the result of seeds I had sown in my life. It would have been easier to blame my ex-husband, circumstances, or some other thing rather than face the reality that the choices I made had a cause and effect relationship with the end result of a divorce.

Absolute honesty is required if you want to learn to sow better results in the future.

The Law of Increase has to do with your thoughts and your speech and the impact they have on your environment. During a time of economic downturn, it is easy to become discouraged and negative. Voicing your worries and fears reinforces your negative thoughts. Choose your thoughts and your words carefully, particularly at work or in your business. Your words are the tool you use to create your future. In her book *Every Word Has Power*, Yvonne Oswald explains how words shape our minds and our futures. The conversations we have with ourselves are the most important. It is possible to reframe our language by switching negative-low energy words to positive—high energy words. A few words that Oswald suggests we switch would include:

- Speak in the present tense whenever possible. ("It's easy to have a relationship now" rather than "I will have a relationship.")
- Add a health connection to plans and goals to incorporate the unconscious mind's interest in preserving your health and well-being. ("My new class schedule is great because I will have plenty of time to relax in the afternoons.")
- Use the words "because" and "now" as often as possible because it provides the reason why, causing the unconscious mind to take action.
- Switch the word "don't" in sentences. ("Don't trip!" becomes "Watch your step!")
- Clear "have to", "could have" and "should" from your vocabulary.
- Clear the word "try" from your vocabulary.
- Change the word "but" to the word "and" in your sentences. ("That's a great job, but you need to correct this mistake" becomes "That's a great job and here's how it can be even better.")
- Use words that empower and build, such as gratitude, joy, abundance, love, freedom, power, health, laughter, kindness, success.[15]

The Universal Law of Giving and Receiving

Abundance is based on a dynamic flow in and through our lives. We have compared it to a river that cannot be controlled on command, but can be turned in the direction we wish. Another analogy would be the flow of blood through the human body. Stop that flow, and blood clots. Without proper circulation of blood the body dies. **Life requires the flow of energy. Giving and receiving is one way to create that dynamic movement**. When wealth or resources come into your life, a portion of that abundance needs to be given away to maintain the flow. Hanging on to resources is evidence of a scarcity mentality. To experience affluence, you must allow resources to move in and out of your life. The very word "affluence" comes from a Latin word that means "to flow to."

When scarcity grips the heart of someone, they are fearful that they will not have enough. They react to this fear by hanging on to what they have. This hanging on stops the flow and creates the lack of resources they were afraid of in the first place. No matter how small your paycheck, look for ways to give if you want to bring more abundance into your life. You do not have to give money to practice the Law of Giving and Receiving. You can give your time, your skills, even something as simple as a smile or a prayer. It is the mindset of giving that is important.

> *"I give away my time, my skills, my network of friends, my life experience. You do not need money to be a philanthropist. We all have assets. You can befriend life with your bare hands."*
>
> *Rachel Remen, MD*

I was raised in a family with a high value for giving above and beyond the traditional tithe. A tithe is traditionally ten percent of your income, and it is usually given to the organization that ministers to you spiritually. I had been taught that the tithe was the bare minimum I ought to be giving. As a young teen I watched my father give even when he was laid off from his job. During those months my dad shared with our family how abundance seemed to flow whenever he would give, and that he received more back than he ever gave away. When I first started my business, cash flow was limited. I had just enough to cover my expenses, so I decided to give away my time and talents. I did some research and found the House of Hope. The House of Hope is a place where women can go when they need support, encouragement, guidance and shelter. Because of my experience of being homeless and needy at one point in my life, I decided this was where I wanted to give of my resources. The Law of Giving and Receiving was impressed on me in such a powerful way as a result of this decision. In order to volunteer at the House, you are required to take a class called the Ultimate Journey. The material in this class was just what I needed to learn how to challenge the lies and self-limiting beliefs I carried from my childhood and the experiences I had in my first marriage. It was such a healing experience. I went to the House to give and ended up receiving much more than I could ever imagine. This is how the Law of Giving and Receiving works.

You can never out give God. It doesn't matter if you give a tithe of ten percent, or more or less—just give. Give to the people and places that have touched your life.

The Law of Reciprocity is closely related to the Law of Giving. **When you give, others are highly motivated to give back**. Sales and marketing executives make use of the Law of Reciprocity all the time. Free samples motivate many to purchase products they hadn't planned to buy. A pharmaceutical sales representative gets her foot in the door at a medical practice by bringing the nurses and doctors lunch. That "free" lunch compels the doctors to give the saleswoman valuable time to pitch her products. Neighbors and friends sometimes operate under the Law of Reciprocity: I buy you lunch or bring you baked goods and then you return the favor.

Robert Cialdini refers to a study on reciprocity in his book *Yes! 50 Scientifically Proven Ways to be Persuasive*. In this study, social psychologist Dennis Regan conducted an experiment where people were given a small gift of a can of Coca Cola. After a period of time the man who gave them the gift approached them to buy raffle tickets, but didn't say anything about the can of Coca Cola. The people who received the can of Coke purchased twice as many raffle tickets as people who did not receive any gift.[16] Reciprocity ensures that abundance flows back to you when you give, even when you give with the intention of getting back in return.

The Law of Giving and Receiving also incorporates the Law of Love and Good Will. This law has a very different motivation that the Law of Reciprocity. In the Law of Love, you give unconditionally, without any expectation of receiving. Your gift is intended to be a blessing to others. The Hebrew word "chesed" captures the essense of this concept and is translated as "loving-kindness." Chesed is central to Jewish theology and considered by many to be a primary virtue. The best gifts often have nothing to do with money. When giving in love, the gift might be a note, a compliment, a prayer, or a silent blessing. In *The 7 Spiritual Laws of Success*, Deepak Choprah challenges us to never visit anyone empty-handed. He teaches that bearing gifts everywhere keeps the flow of abundance circulating. Offering love and affection to others is one of the best ways to bring abundance into your life.

Receiving is an important part of the Law of Giving and Receiving. It is difficult for some to receive gifts and blessings from others. This wall of resistance often comes from a sense of pride and the desire to be known as someone who meets their own needs. The failure to receive from others stops the flow of abundance. Being a grateful, gracious receiver takes practice. Blessing others by receiving their gifts will keep abundance circulating through your life.

> *"The universe operates through dynamic exchange . . . giving and receiving are different aspects of the flow of energy in the universe. And in our willingness to give that which we seek, we keep the abundance of the universe circulating in our lives."*
>
> *Deepak Chopra*

The Universal Law of Persistence

> *"Nothing in the world can take the place of persistence. Talent will not; nothing is more common than unsuccessful men with talent. Education will not; the world is full of*

> *educated derelicts. Persistence and determination alone are omnipotent. The slogan "Press on" has solved and always will solve the problems of the human race."*
>
> *Calvin Coolidge*

The difference between success and failure is persistence. Throughout this book you have seen calls to action. Taking action, one step at a time, is the only way to see results. And once you have started taking action, persistence is required to see you through to the end. Persistence will not take "no" for an answer. To "persist" literally means "to refuse to give up." **Persistence will see you through to abundance.**

Persistence is the mindset that you can and will succeed. When times get hard and discouragement sets in, your persistence is tested. Those who are able to coach themselves into staying the course win the race. There is discipline in persistence: A discipline of mind that focuses on the end result regardless of the pain, set-backs, disappointments and defeats.

In the years prior to World War II, Winston Churchill was mocked and ridiculed for his opinions on Nazi Germany. He was one of a few politicians who saw the danger growing in Europe and urged Parliament to act. Churchill lost position and power, but persisted in sounding the alarm. Once war was declared, Churchill was vindicated and given a powerful role in history because of his determination to "Never give in; never, never give in."

Patty was a client of mine who loves wine. She was great at dreaming up unique wine and food pairings. She left a corporate job to pursue her passion and sell wine in a network marketing company. Success in network marketing requires two skill sets: selling product and recruiting new sales representatives. Patty was great at selling the product, but she really struggled with building a sales team. This challenge was affecting her income. After working at her business for a few months, her husband started to worry that she would never replace her corporate salary. Nearly every day he would ask her if she thought she should go back to her old job. This constant negativity from her husband was draining to Patty, but she wanted to work with wine and stuck with her business.

Patty and I started working together to see if she could build a team and create the kind of business that would make her husband to sit up and take notice. She worked hard to develope skills and began to see results. Her income went up as her team grew, and Patty began winning awards with her company for recruiting and sales. When she was able to take her husband on vacation, he admitted that his suggestions that she quit were premature. He became Patty's biggest supporter. Everything seemed to be going marvelously when it all came crashing down.

The owner of the company Patty worked for sold his part of the company and new ownership stepped in to make changes. Almost overnight the company began to fall apart. Patty, who had risen to a leadership position, met with other leaders to talk about what to do. Many were ready to throw in the towel and walk away. Patty wondered if she was going to have to go back to her old job after all. Fear started to creep into her heart, but she persisted. Even when members of her team left and the company looked like it was going to crumble, Patty hung on. She had a vision of helping the company turn around and become even better than before. And that is just what happened. The new owner of the company left, the former owner returned, and new systems were put in place that improved compensation and benefits for the sales representatives. Because of her persistence, Patty was rewarded with leadership and respect from her colleagues. She loved her job and pursued her passions.

"Failure is success trying to be born in a bigger way."
Catherine Ponder

Failure and fear are no reason to give up your dream of living a passionate, abundant life. Patty learned to be persistent, even when everyone around her had doubts about her success. If you are following a clear plan of action and pursuing your passion, persistence will pay off.

The Universal Law of Creativity

Anthony Robbins says that there is no lack of resources, just resourcefulness. **The Universal Law of Creativity taps into your imagination to create a pathway for abundance**. There is no limit to what you can do. Your mind is virtually an untapped resource as you have millions of brain cells you never use. Studies show that the average man or woman only uses about one percent of the potential available in the brain. Just imagine what you could do if you put this untapped resource to work.

Years ago a computer took up an entire room because of the space required for all the circuits and processors. When the microchip was created, computers began to get smaller and smaller. They also began to get faster and have much more capacity to store information. Computers advanced as microchips and processors began being combined to work together, maximizing output exponentially. Imagine the tiniest computer the size of the head on a pin. That computer is a brain cell. Your brain is filled with millions of tiny micro-processors that have the capability of communicating with one another, storing information, and generating output. Your mind controls this amazing biological machine. You have the ability not only to dream up innovative solutions, but also to implement them and profit from them. If you need more money, time, health or any other resource, you can put your mind to work to solve the problem.

One of my favorite ways to unlock creativity is to have conversations with myself about the problem at hand. If the problem is in my business, I imagine having a talk with my business and asking it for suggestions on what to do. A few years ago I created an assessment tool for businesses and needed to figure out how to get the word out that it was available. I asked my "business" what it would suggest I do to market this new tool. Immediately the answer came: "Offer to let your former and current clients try the tool out for free, and then ask them to tell other business owners about it." I know this solution actually came from my own mind, but it seemed as if the answer came from my business. I actually used the strategy I came up with in my imaginary conversation, and it worked extremely well.

A similar technique involves asking an expert for advice in an imaginary conversation. Imagine you are asking Einstein for help on a physics problem or Jonas Salk about a medical issue. When I'm struggling with my attitude toward others, I consult with Mother Teresa of Calcutta. When I want sales advice and motivation I talk to Brian Tracy. The fascinating thing about these conversations is the quality of the advice you get. You are consulting with you own mind, engaging your own brain, and coming up with unique solutions to problems.

A technique that has proven powerful for me and my clients is something I call "The Brain Dump". At the top of a piece of paper or a white board you write your question. It might be a question like: "How can I raise $5,000 by this Friday?" After you write this question down, take a moment to clear your mind of distractions. Set a timer for 15 minutes, take a deep breath, and then write down as many answers as you possibly can. Your answers can be outrageous or realistic. Avoid filtering while you write. Stop when the timer goes off and review your list. Consider every option and how it might be implemented. Write the viable options on a new piece of paper. If you don't have two or three viable options, set the timer and go again for 15 minutes. Write as fast as you can and let your imagination take flight. After two or three rounds of generating options, you will find yourself considering new alternatives that never occurred to you before. When you review your lists, consider how combining options can create new options. The key to successfully completing 'The Brain Dump' is that you select one option and take immediate action. There is something about taking quick action that reinforces your brain. You teach yourself to take yourself seriously. Use the POWER acronym described in Chapter 1 to find creative solutions:

P — Define the **problem**.

What am I trying to create? What purpose would it serve?

O—Consider all your **options**.

What are all the possible ways I could solve this problem? What has and has not be done?

W— **Work** on the problem using one of the options.

Try out one of the options from above and see how it works.

E— **Evaluate** your progress or success.

Test your progress and results by asking others for input on your creation.

R— **Review** the process, **Revise** if necessary, and **Reward** yourself.

Does your finished product solve the problem you intended to solve? If not, does it solve another important problem? You may have something worthwhile. If you have not solved your original problem, is it still pressing? What do you need to do to refine your process? Can you revise, or do you need to go back and select another option? If you have solved your problem, or are satisfied with your outcome, CELEBRATE YOUR SUCCESS!

The more you get into a habit of using these types of techniques, the greater your capacity for creative problem solving will be.

Give yourself permission to want, to dream, to desire. Listen to your heart and free the passions living there. The Bible tell us that God gives us the desires of our heart. Some take that to mean that God delivers what we want. What it actually means is that the desires themselves are Divine. Do you want to travel? Does your heart yearn for strange new places or beautiful new landscapes? There is a reason and a purpose behind those desires that you may not be aware of.

What dreams are in your heart? Let yourself imagine things that seem impossible. Then get to work to make it happen.

A Personal Lesson

For several years after starting my coaching practice money was very tight. As a single woman I not only had to cover my business expenses, but also had to make enough to cover rent, utilities, and groceries. There were times that I wasn't sure I was going to make it. I lived with the fear of getting sick or having my car break down because I didn't have anything set aside for emergencies. I never considered the option of closing my practice and taking a 'job' (I'll explain why in the chapter on Purpose), but these were tough times.

One day I hit rock bottom. I was down to my last six dollars. I had written checks against all the money I had in the bank. I had six dollars cash in my wallet and that was it. I was so discouraged. I had been working hard to build my practice, and it just seemed as though I was getting nowhere financially. I remember debating with myself whether I should go to a meeting across town. My tank was full of gas and the meeting didn't cost anything. I decided I needed to be around people, even if I wasn't telling anyone how bad things were. As I drove, I remember praying and asking God to help me know what to do. This wasn't the first conversation I had with God about my situation, but this time I prayed expecting an answer. I felt prompted to take the money out of my wallet and lay it on the passenger seat. I continued driving and praying, and as I thought about my income and expenses I had a startling realization. **I had more than I needed.** I had enough money in the bank to cover the checks I'd written to pay my bills. I had food in my cupboards at home. I had clothing and toiletries. I had a full tank of gas in my car. I even had plenty of dog food. The six dollars lying on the seat next to me was more than I needed.

I pulled over and stopped to thank God for each of those six dollars. I asked Him to multiply each dollar and to do so in way that I would recognize His hand at work. When I finished praying, I put my money back in my purse and went to my meeting.

While at the meeting, my friends asked me about a speaker's bureau that I had been considering joining. I had put off joining because of my financial situation, but I didn't want to tell my friends how broke I was. I tried to change the subject, but one friend persisted and made me promise that I would contact the speaker's bureau and join by the end of the week. I was going to make another excuse when I had a realization: the membership fees and cost of the portfolio I needed for the speaker's bureau came to $600. In my heart I told God this would be a great way to step up and multiply my six dollars. In faith, I told my friend I would follow through that week.

On the way home I received a phone call from a man inquiring about my coaching services. He told me he had been reading articles I'd written and checking out my website for six weeks. He was ready to hire me right there on the spot without any sales pitch. He had worked with several big name coaches and I was stunned that he had called me. He told me what he had been paying his last coach and asked if I would be willing to charge the same fee. I tried to keep my voice from squeaking when I said, "Sure, that would be fine." The amount he offered to pay me was $3,000 more than my regular rate for 3 months of coaching. Then he blew me away and agreed to work with me for six months. Six months of coaching for $6,000 more than my regular rate. Even better, he paid me while we were on the phone using Paypal, so I had the money in my account before I even got home.

Over the next two weeks, five more new clients hired me, making a total of six new clients. That same month I got a contract to do training for a company for $600. And then as if all this weren't enough, God made me laugh out loud when an envelope arrived in the mail containing a stock payment from a former employer. The check was for 66 cents. My prayer of faith was answered with such abundance that I couldn't help but recognize the Source.

My lesson in abundance was simple. **Abundance means more than enough**. It doesn't necessarily mean wealth. You can have an abundant life living in a simple home, driving a reliable car, with just enough money to cover your expenses with a little extra at the end of the month. You have a choice to live with an abundance mentality when it comes to your health, your wealth, your time and every other resource imaginable. Shift your mindset with gratitude and humility and you will begin to appreciate abundance.

EXERCISES for Appreciating Abundance

1. Radical Gratitude

We often don't appreciate things until we don't have them. Take a few minutes to practice radical gratitude for everything you can think of, down to the smallest detail in your life. It may be for the health of your fingernails, the fact that your refrigerator works, or for the way your dog wags his tail when you enter the room. Make a list of 100 things you are grateful for in your life.

2. A Gratitude Practice

Create a gratitude practice that you use every day for a month. Your practice might be doing the Radical Gratitude exercise every day. Or you might borrow my practice:

Thank God for five things you are grateful for. Then tell God the five things you are handing off because they are too big for you to carry. Finally, thank God for the five things you anticipate feeling grateful for—and word your prayer as if you already have them.

3. Why Aren't You Rich?

Take out a piece of paper and write down all the things that are keeping you from abundance in your life. You might realize that you don't have as much money as you could because you have been paying bank fees on returned checks because you don't balance your checkbook regularly. Or maybe you aren't experiencing an abundance of help at work because you haven't asked for it. Review your list and choose one item to take action on immediately.

4. Money Journal

Begin a money journal that tracks the stories and lessons you are learning about abundance. My story about the six dollars came from my money journal. I would not have learned this lesson if I hadn't been paying attention. Journaling will increase your awareness of what you are learning.

5. Family History

Track your family tree back to your grandparents or even your great-grandparents, and consider what type of lives they led and what their attitudes about abundance might have been. Did they enjoy robust health? Did they have more than enough money? Were they well-respected in their communities and enjoy an abundance of influence? Reflect on how your family has influenced your beliefs about abundance and determine to shift beliefs that are not working for you.

6. Asset Inventory

What are the assets that you value the most? Create an inventory of your physical assets, and as you list them, say a word of thanks for each item. Then move on to intangible assets: your education, experience, talents, and strengths. Count your relationships, including your network of professional contacts. Recognize just how wealthy you are as you consider all your assets.

7. Serve Others

One of the best ways to increase appreciation for what you have is to serve those who are suffering from lack of abundance. Volunteer at a food bank, a community health center, or mission outreach. Read to a child at a school in a needy neighborhood. Work on a Habitat for Humanity home.

8. Clear Some Space

- What area in your life could use more abundance? Clear some space in that area.

- Are you struggling with coming up with new content or ideas at work? Clear your desk.
- Do you want better health? Clear your body of toxins by going on a juice and water fast for a day or two.
- Do you wish you had nicer furniture? Clear the clutter and all of the old, broken things out of your home.
- Do you feel like you need more time in your day? Delegate activities that others could do for you.

Get creative! Clear some space and watch abundance flow.

9. Above and Beyond

Choose an organization or individual who has fed your spirit and begin to give on a regular basis. Give above and beyond a tithe. Give joyfully and with gratitude for what you have received. Determine to give as much as you can, and watch to see how it comes back to you.

10. Wish List

Create a wish list or vision board of the things that represent abundance to you. For me, having financial freedom means that I have discretionary income after all the bills are paid and I've given to my faith community. If I have more than enough, that means I have great sheets and towels. Several years ago I put a picture of a linen closet full of beautiful sheets and towels on a vision board. Right after my husband and I got married we gave away all our old sheets and towels and started out with new, gorgeous Egyptian cotton linens. Coincidence? Believe what you want, but I know I feel richer sleeping on these gorgeous sheets!

CHAPTER 8

FINDING FAITH

[fāTH] Confident belief in the truth, value, or trustworthiness of a person, idea, or thing; belief that does not rest on logical proof or material; **a strong belief in a supernatural power or powers that influence human destiny.**

"Now faith is the substance of things hoped for, the evidence of things not seen."
Hebrews 11:1

The word faith makes a lot of people nervous. For some it conjures up images of religious gatherings and dogma. For others the word is wrapped in clouds of elusive mysteries and ideas that are far too "out there" to be anything more than "touchy-feely-woo-woo". For still others faith is a gauntlet thrown down by a challenger requiring them to take a leap into the unknown without a safety net in order to win the prize. The kind of faith discussed in this chapter is all of those things and none of them. Faith creates confidence where uncertainty exists. Faith drives us forward to do things we never thought we could. Faith is founded firmly on truth and gives us a boldness that overrides our fears.

There are several kinds of faith including an acknowledgement of God's existence, a system of moral and religious teachings, a trusting or trustworthiness, and a belief that drives behavior due to complete surrender to mental acceptance of an idea. All of these types of faith are valid and important, but it is this last definition that is the focus of this chapter.

Faith is an internal belief that does not rely on external evidence for confirmation. The abstract nature of faith makes it easier for some to trust and harder for others because of basic personality differences. About 75% of the population prefers to take in information through their senses. The Myers-Briggs Type Indicator calls this group Sensors (S). They prefer concrete information they can touch, feel, taste, or smell. They are more comfortable with facts and figures than abstract ideas or metaphors. The other 25% of the population use their senses, but prefer to trust intuition and hunches rather than depend on hard cold facts. This group of abstract thinkers is called iNtuitive (N) on the Myers-Briggs (with a capital N because of another trait, Introvert, uses the capital I).[1] Karen Armstrong describes this difference as a preference for Logos or Mythos. Both preferences are essential to humanity, offering important perspectives. Neither is considered superior but are regarded as complimentary, each with its special area of competence. Logos is "rational, pragmatic, and scientific thought" where Mythos "was not concerned with practical matters, but with meaning".[2] The words "myth" and "mysticism" both stem from the Greek *musteion*: to close the mouth or the eyes.[3] These words are associated with experiences that are silent, obscure, and not rationally demonstrable. These dramatic differences in temperament between the Sensor/Logos and the Intuitive/Mythos make faith a challenging subject to explain in a way satisfying for everyone. As you read this chapter, knowing your basic personality type will be helpful. If you are an S on the Myers-Briggs, it will also be helpful for you to know that this author is a very strong N. Be patient with me and keep an open mind as I will be sharing very practical aspects of finding and living by faith.

For centuries faith was left to the religious to decipher and explore. Living by faith became associated with religious teachings. In more recent years people have come to understand that while faith is certainly the subject of study among religious groups and churches, a religious institution is not the only place and is not necessarily the best place to learn how to live by faith. Faith needs to be worked out in everyday life. It is the application of faith to the day to day challenges we face that increase our capacity for growth, success, and even greater faith.

Faith is a spiritual concept, not in the religious sense, but in the sense that it does not reside in the body or the mind. Humans are made up of body, soul (mind) and spirit, and respond to situations in their environment through each at different times. Napoleon Hill, in *Think and Grow Rich*, spoke of these three aspects of man. He described how sexual responses came from the body, calculations came from the mind, and faith came from the spirit. Hill was adamant on the necessity of developing faith in order to have success in life and business.[4] It is possible to have a deep spiritual connection without a religious agenda. Beware of rejecting the idea of finding faith because of reservations you have about religion.

Faith recognizes that you can take action, even when the path or outcome is unclear. Faith acknowledges that you are not alone on your journey, that there is a higher power at work supporting, guiding, directing. On the continuum of faith you find paralyzing fear at one end and arrogant ego at the other. It is ego that says you have no need for faith—in God or anyone else.

Egoism

The ego is one's sense of self. Ego is necessary for self-identity, self-esteem, and a healthy level of self-autonomy. We need this autonomy as we move from childhood dependence to healthy self-reliance. It is important to have a healthy ego, but all too often we focus on building up ego without strengthening the balancing aspects of our personality, particularly faith. Faith requires that we move away from ego's self-serving focus. Ego says "I can do it all myself". Ego believes it can succeed on its own and wants the credit for that success. Faith says "I am empowered by a Power beyond myself to do whatever it takes to succeed."

> *"Independent of your race, gender, culture, social status, education, religious beliefs, or even past mistakes, there is a power within each of us that is common to every human being—and we are all connected to it."*
>
> *Joe Dispenza*

Faith recognizes that we cannot go it alone, that we need something or SomeOne beyond ourselves to fulfill our purpose. The Ego wants to make its own rules and forge its own way. It needs to have power over others, to be the best, and to be in control. Faith accepts the need for mastery without control. Faith is the confidence that God [The Universe, Source, Spirit] daily conspires for our good. A leap of faith is essential for growth. The Spirit says "leap", but the mind behind the Ego says "no, wait, don't do it, we need more facts". The scriptures teach us that "Faith is the substance of things hoped for, the evidence of things unseen."[5] Faith is the reality behind the scenes. Egoism is driven by the rational mind. Faith, on the other hand, is at the mercy of the soul. To live by faith means we have resigned ourselves to the Power that is beyond our reach. When we pursue faith we realize life and reality beyond our current existence.

> *"Look, his* ego *is inflated; he is without integrity. But the righteous one will live by his* faith.*"*
>
> *Habakkuk 2:4*

Fear

When the ego is threatened with a loss of control it will throw up emotional roadblocks of fear. While Ego says "I can do it myself", Fear says "I can't do anything." Fear cringes at the thought of moving forward without clear proof and safety, but once fear has set in no amount of proof can move it. Fear is not rational and attempts to reason with it are futile. It can cause physical reactions, and you might sense fear as a queasy stomach, a pressure headache, or even a flush or rash on your skin. The pain and discomfort created by fear is hard to remove, often because we do not want to admit we are afraid. Like all negative beliefs, your brain will try to hang on to your fear out of a misguided sense of protection. Fear can only be overcome with faith.

When the idea to leave my job to create my own business came, I rejected it immediately out of fear. How would I support myself? What if I couldn't build a clientele fast enough? What about health insurance? All kinds of questions around "how would I" and "what if" bombarded me every time the thought popped into my mind. It was hard to give any serious thought to creating a plan when so many questions were unanswered. I thought these questions were rational and important enough to delay taking action. Months later I was complaining about my job to a trusted friend and he said, "You know what is wrong with this situation? You're an entrepreneur. You are never going to be happy working for someone else. What is keeping you from starting your own business?" He then began outlining all the gifts I had to offer and ways I could serve others while working for myself. As he spoke, I felt the questions that had been holding me back popping like bubbles. They were based on fear, not facts. I needed to take action and face those fears with faith. I took a leap of faith to start the business that led me to write this book. It has not always been easy, but I wouldn't trade those lean years for anything. The lessons I learned about living by faith were necessary, laying a foundation for every leap of faith I would have to take to succeed.

Faith is built step by step. You learn to live by faith every time you step into positive proof. Standing on positive proof means reminding yourself of all the times you did this or something similar. This requires a mind shift, for we are unfortunately wired to focus on all the proof we've gathered to the contrary. In *The Firestarter Sessions*, Danielle LaPorte suggests that you ought to "remember everything you've ever done or has happened to you in your entire life and the history of humankind has brought you to this point—that's a whole lot of life force on your side."[6] Faith holds a deaf ear to the voices in our heads and in our environments that tells us to stop, to give up, to wait, or to hold back.

How is fear holding you back from the life you were designed to lead? What would you do if you knew you could not fail? If specific ideas and dreams came to mind as a result of those questions, you would benefit from replacing fear with faith.

Run Toward the Lions

'What are you afraid of?' is a very powerful question. Coaches frequently ask it because so often people are paralyzed by fear and don't even recognize it. When it came to writing this book, I knew exactly what I was afraid of: "What will people think?" That question and the speculative answers I created were powerful enough to paralyze me over and over again. I am embarrassed to admit how long it took me to finish this book because of all the times I stopped and started and stopped again because of fear.

I was frustrated with myself over being stuck on a specific section of writing one morning and shared this with my friend and *Passion Test for Business* mentor Beth Lefevre.

"Run toward your fear," she said.

"What?" I asked.

"Run toward your fear. Moving in the direction of your fear will save you. You've heard the story about the old lions, right?" I could hear Beth smiling through the phone.

"I don't think so . . ." I was confused.

"There is an old African story about how a pride of lions hunt together, circling their prey. The group will come upon an antelope and at one end of the circle, you will find the old lions with their tired joints and dull teeth. These old lions have a ferocious roar. When they begin to roar, the terrified antelope runs away from the roar—right into the jaws of the young lions waiting at the other end of the circle. The young lions are fast and their teeth are sharp—and you never hear them until it's too late. The antelope that runs toward their fear have a much greater chance of survival. So, run toward your fear."

We talked more about my specific fear. My greatest fear was that people will read what I've written and think, "Wow—I thought she was [smarter / deeper / more Christian / more open-minded / a better writer] than that!" You can fill in the blank with your own criticism, whatever it might be. I'm sure you get the point. I was afraid it wouldn't be good enough. But running toward the fear meant that I needed to sit down and write what was in my heart regardless of what others might think. Instead of shriveling up, I had to boldly face these imaginary critics and tell them they don't get to tear my work apart—particularly before it was even finished!

Another piece of wisdom about writing fears came from Christine Kloser, founder of the Transformational Author's Experience. Christine counsels her clients to "Listen to your Truth voice, not your trash voice." The truth lies in your heart, particularly when you are writing. Both Beth and Christine helped me realize that I wasn't writing for the critics, but for the men and women around the globe who wanted and needed to hear what is in my heart. Embracing this audience made it much easier to run toward my fear!

What are YOU afraid of? Run toward your fear. Be bold and know that the old lions will never be able to catch you as long as you keep moving!

Faith

We've stated that faith is not ego or fear, but what exactly is faith and how do we develop it? Early in this chapter we said that **faith is a belief that drives behavior due to the complete surrender to mental acceptance of an idea.** Let's unpack this definition phrase by phrase and outline just how to find and increase faith.

Acceptance

First, faith is a belief. A belief is an **acceptance** that a statement is true or that something exists. Faith requires acceptance. When you are faced with a challenge, don't fight it—faith it. Bathe that challenge in the belief that this challenge has purpose for you right this moment or it wouldn't be present in your life. Receive the challenge and look within for the resources you've already been given to overcome it. Faith is that glimmer of hope and confidence that everything will turn out right. Fan the flames of faith in your heart and don't let the naysayers pour cold water on it or smother it.

Action

Next, faith is driven by behavior. In other words, faith takes **action** based on acceptance that something is true. Once you have decided to accept the challenge and have identified the resources you will use, the next step is to outline the path you will take and step forward. All too often we see men and women who sense a calling to do something new or different, but they never move toward that vision. They spend a great deal of time talking, thinking, and planning, but fail to do the one thing that takes them closer to success. The smallest step forward will overcome inertia and create the momentum you need to complete the task. We often can't see where the second step is or where all the resources will come from until we begin to move forward.

Surrender

Faith involves complete **surrender**. To surrender is to cease resistance. Acceptance was the first phase of surrender. When you decided that this challenge had purpose and meaning at this point in your life, you began to surrender to your destiny. In my faith experience, I have seen evidence over and over again of a Power at work in my life. I like to think of this Power as the Master Musician composing and orchestrating every note. When I pay attention to the Conductor's baton, I stay in rhythm, enter at the right point, and stop when it's time to be still. As a member of the orchestra, I must study my part and rehearse, but I need the guidance of the Conductor to direct me to my best performance. Watching for direction, listening intently, following the slightest invitation to act is necessary to complete the beautiful work of art you were designed to create. Surrendering to faith does not mean laying back and letting things just happen. Surrender in this case means yielding control in order to move with the flow of life, open to the shifts and changes that come.

Back to Acceptance

Finally, faith requires mental acceptance of an idea. Faith brings us back around to accepting more new and different ideas. Faith opens our hearts to possibilities and to greater clarity about the truth. The faith journey is a spiral that winds upward, returning back to similar ground, but never on exactly the same path. We face and relearn some of the same lessons over and over again, not necessarily because we failed to learn them the first time, but because we are now equipped to go deeper.

> *"The journey of surrender is one of continuing to trust that all is happening in divine perfect order . . . all the time. When you disconnect from living in a surrendered place—and lose sight of the larger perspective of your soul's true journey—that is when fear and doubt can creep in. So, allow yourself to enjoy a few moments today to re-commit to surrendering your personal will (as well as your fears) and riding on the wings of grace instead."*
>
> *Christine Kloser*

Looking back at my leap of faith when I started my business, I first had to believe in the truth that I was meant to start my own business. Opening up to a new idea is difficult, but as I began to let myself consider the idea, I began to see opportunities and possibilities unfold. Next I needed to take action. When I began moving in the direction of starting my own business, I began to gain confidence. The fear-filled questions that had blocked my taking action before shriveled in the presence of faith-filled action and assurance. And finally, when I surrendered to the idea, I stopped generating questions. Instead I started generating reasons why I should work for myself rather than all the reasons why I shouldn't. As I moved forward, I faced similar challenges as the first time I worked for myself. Even though the challenges were similar, I was not the same person. I generated new ideas and went in a very different direction. New solutions and possibilities presented themselves, and I found myself stretching and growing. Success was easier this time around, because I operated in faith instead of fear.

Acceptance, surrender and action are not words that feed the ego or fear. Letting go of preconceived notions and the noise generated by fear is something that must be practiced and mastered. We have examples of great leaders and spiritual teachers who have demonstrated this process. Abraham Lincoln was a dismal failure in politics, but he did not give in to ego or fear, went on to run for the highest office in the United States and became one of our most loved presidents. Mahatma Gandhi spoke of filling his mind with truth and peace to avoid the fear, doubt and unbelief that would have derailed his leading his country to freedom. Jesus Christ, in spite of incredible temptation and opposition, did "only that which pleases the Father" and demonstrated a life of faith and surrender.

"Uncommon faith yields uncommon results."

Joel Osteen

Marcy Puts Faith to Work

Marcy had come a long way in rebuilding her beliefs. She had strengthened her resilience, repaired and reinforced her connections, and practiced taking initiative without the perfectionism that once plagued her. She was beginning to experience abundance in her work and her family life. Faith was not an issue—or so we thought until she began to have health problems. Marcy was disciplined in maintaining a healthy diet, getting enough sleep, and managing her stress. There didn't seem to be any explanation for the overwhelming fatigue that landed her in the doctor's office for tests. A serious iron deficiency with no known source made her physician suspect cancer. Marcy began to worry about her kids, her business, her finances, and her future. Everything depended on her being healthy enough to keep her business going. She was not yet at the point where the business could run without her. What was she going to do if she really was sick?

Fear began eating away at Marcy's heart. She began to question why she needed to continue to work so hard if it was all going to go away since she was dying. In her mind, Marcy had gone from feeling tired to already being dead and buried. She began to feel angry. She had worked so hard. Was it all for nothing? Her ego resented all the bills that were piling up as medical tests were run to find the cancer the doctors suspected; her ego insisted that she demand answers immediately. Marcy is a deeply spiritual person, but prayer was not a comfort to her during this time. She didn't understand why God seemed shut off from her.

Marcy's childhood training had taught her that negative emotions like anger, worry and fear are sin. When someone believes their spiritual connection is at risk, they will deny and repress these normal negative emotions. We were designed to experience both positive and negative emotions. By themselves, they are not sin, but rather signals that we have let go of faith. Even when times seem dark, when discouragement sets in, we must hang on to faith. It is often the only light on the path to freedom and joy. When Marcy was challenged with this concept, she stopped questioning "Why me" and "What if". She began to trust that everything would work out, not because she was in control, but because God was.

It doesn't matter whether you believe in God the way Marcy does. It doesn't matter what you call the Source, the Creator, the Universe, Spirit—He / She / It believes in you. That Creative Force is in control of your destiny and the final outcome. You can't control things like the weather, the stock market, or cancer. But the Source of All That Is can and does. Placing your faith in the One who holds your destiny in the palm of His hand is easy when you consider the alternative.

Marcy knew that her prayers had been blocked by her lack of faith. God had been hearing her, but she had stopped listening to Him. It was just after she had this epiphany when she got a call about the most recent set of tests. The doctors had determined that Marcy did not have cancer, but that her system simply absorbed iron extraordinarily slowly. She was not dying, but simply needed to take large doses of iron supplements and wait.

When Marcy called with her news that she was going to be just fine, she shared something interesting. "If I hadn't been forced to think about how to run my business if I was sick, I wouldn't have come up with solutions for problems that have drained me of time and money from day one. Now that I know I'm not sick, I'm going to simplify things, eliminate the energy drains, and focus on what I love doing best." Marcy had been forced into improving her business and was more excited than ever about what the future might hold for her and her children.

Marcy stepped out in faith in her life and her business. She has accepted the challenges she faces in her business and surrendered to the lessons she needs to learn. She took action, putting systems in place that will make her business more productive and less dependent on her active involvement. She found creative solutions that promise to make her business even more successful.

"Every set back is a set up for a greater come back."

T. D. Jakes

Even the most spiritually minded people can struggle with finding faith in tough times. A life of faith leaves us feeling very vulnerable, but vulnerability is a strength all its own. Stepping out into the unknown and trusting what is in our hearts gives us incredible power.

"Never doubt in the darkness that which you believed in the light."

Stephen R. Lawhead

Faith and Success

Think and Grow Rich was written in 1937 and continues to be considered relevant today—often called the "grandfather of all motivational books". In it, Napoleon Hill had much to say on the subject of faith. **"Faith is the only agency through which the cosmic force of infinite intelligence can be harnessed and used by humanity . . . Whatever the mind can conceive and believe, it can achieve."** Hill wrote about how our minds work on an unconscious level to translate thoughts into reality. Thoughts driven by fear will just as readily become reality as thoughts driven by courage or faith. We get to choose our reality and the world our minds create through our thoughts. Hill challenges us to fill our minds with the things that lead to faith.[7]

> *"Applied faith is the mental attitude where you can clear your mind of all fears and doubts and direct it toward whatever you desire."*
>
> *Napoleon Hill*

In his book *Breaking The Habit of Being Yourself: How to Lose Your Mind and Create a New One,* Dr. Joe Dispenza explains the neuroscience behind what Napoleon Hill described above:

> Because of the size of the human frontal lobe, you have the privilege of making thought more real than anything else. Thus, when you close your eyes and eliminate the barrage of stimuli from your external world, you can formulate a new image of yourself without distraction just by going within. And when you are truly focused and pay attention, there comes a moment when your brain does not know the difference between what is real in the external world and what you imagine in your mind. In fact, the thoughts you are embracing will become just like a real life experience in your mind. The moment this occurs, your brain up-scales its hardware to reflect what you're imaging

> and intentionally thinking about. Consequently when you change your mind, you change your brain, and when you change your brain, you change your mind.[8]

If you have been wishing you had more faith to overcome the challenges you are facing, stop waiting for spiritual awakening and start changing the way you think. While faith is a spiritual concept, it begins and expands in the mind. There is a verse of scripture that says *"So then faith comes by hearing, and hearing by the Word of God."*[9] To transform our minds and find the faith we need, we must constantly fill our thoughts with the vision, concepts and truths that will take us forward.

According to Hill, there are "six forms of riches available to us when we master our minds: sound health, peace of mind, labor of love, freedom from fear and worry, positive mental attitude, and riches of your own choice and quantity."[10] Even though all this is available to us, most people go through life in misery because of where they place their focus. The main difference between success and failure is that successful people have a capacity for faith. Failures see only the hole in the donut, but the successful see the hole and the donut around the hole because their eyes are open through faith. Seeing the complete picture, the donut and the hole will give you the ability to see your way to success. Thomas Edison is frequently used as an example of this principle. He failed over and over before finding the solution to his invention. His persistence and his ability to finally see the solution came because he believed there was a solution to be found. How many times will we fail before we give up, or before we push through to success? How long will it take us to choose to develop faith?

EXERCISES for Finding Faith

1. Create Your Credo

A credo is a statement of beliefs that drive you to action. Below is Danielle LaPorte's "A Credo for Making It Happen". Read through these statements and then create your own credo.

A Credo for Making It Happen

1. "I'll figure it out" is the mantra of choice. Accordingly, this buzz kill must be stricken from the lexicon: "I just don't know what to do."
2. If you've never done it before, remember that everything you've ever done or has happened to you in your entire life and the history of humankind has brought you to this point—that's a whole lot of life force on your side.
3. If you've done it before, do it like it's the first time. A beginner's mind is open and an open mind innovates.
4. Respect the fact that doubt is part of the creative process. Examine it as soon as it surfaces. Appreciate that it keeps you alert.
5. Ask yourself what you're going to give up to get where you want to go. You can't have it all or do it all. But you can always have and do great things.
6. Aim for passion, not balance. Balance is a myth. Passion will put your life into the right proportions that work as a whole.
7. Tell people what you're up to. When you declare it and share it you're accountable and helpable.
8. Don't let the desire for perfection become procrastination. Every novel ever written might have been better. Every piece of technology, every masterpiece, every day—it all might have been even better. So just launch and learn.
9. Everything is progress. As any astrophysicist will tell you, the universe is always expanding. That includes you.

10. Do what you say you're going to do. This is the single most powerful behavior for success.
11. Keep it pointed to where you want it to go. Do a little more of what you really want to be doing every day, and a little less of what you don't want to do, until eventually your reality is brimming with the real ideal.

2. Shake Things Up

When you are caught in a cycle of fear or ego, do something that breaks your routine. These negative cycles depend on your feeding them with old patterns of behavior. Find simple ways to shift these patterns, taking baby steps toward the challenge you are facing. If you are afraid of public speaking, introduce yourself to a stranger at a store or at a meeting. If you feel you should be investing in yourself with continuing education but fear tells you that you can't afford it and ego won't ask for help, go to the bank and get a $50 or $100 bill and carry it in your purse or wallet for a few days. Check in with yourself afterwards and see if your perspective or fears have shifted.

3. Take a Cognitive Approach

Use your mind to challenge the negative thoughts and behaviors that keep you from living in faith. For two full weeks, fill in the worksheet below at the end of each day. Notice your feelings, moods, attitudes and write down those negative emotions that are getting in your way.

1. Write down what you have been feeling.
   Example: I felt mildly anxious about attending a meeting where I didn't know anyone and started chewing my nails.

2. Identify where you may have first learned this behavior. Were your parents or caregivers negative, fearful or egotistical?
   Example: My dad used to bite his nails when he was stressed or upset.

3. Look for whatever this emotion has provided for you. How are you benefitting from it? (There is always a pay off!)
   Example: This anxiety has kept me from embarrassing myself in public.

4. Express gratitude for the benefits you've received from these emotions and behavior.
   Example: I am thankful for the anxiety that kept me from embarrassing myself before I was ready to move forward in my career.

5. Release the emotions and behavior by recognizing that you don't need it any more.
   Example: I am ready to let this anxiety go because I am ready to get out and meet people who can help me grow my business.

6. Replace the emotions and behavior with a new productive, constructive, positive habit.
   Example: I am replacing the anxiety with a sense of excitement and anticipation of what I will learn and who I will meet. I am replacing nail biting with sucking a breath mint.

7. Reward yourself with some small thing you appreciate (e.g., time outdoors, a cup of tea, a short video game) when you catch yourself releasing and replacing old emotions and behaviors.
   Example: I am going to allow myself to play 10 minutes of Words With Friends for every time I realize I have replaced anxiety with excitement and nail biting with breath mints.

4. Release Your Attachments

The ego feeds on false attachment. All of us have attachments to people, things and ideas that tie us up instead of supporting us. Follow the steps below to release unhealthy attachments:

1. Create lists of your attachments. Carry these lists around with you for one full week and add to them as necessary.

    - Make a list of people you are attached to in negative ways because of past hurts or wounds, poor boundaries, or dependency.
    - Make a list of things you believe you need to survive.
    - Make a list of luxury items you use every day without gratitude or appreciation, but rather with entitlement or dependence.

2. After you have lived with your lists for a week, review each name or item on your lists and identify the emotions they stir in you. Carry these lists with you for several days and add to them as necessary.
3. Select three of the people or items that generate the most negative emotion for you and use visualization to express all the negative feelings. Do not do this in person, but through imagery.
4. Look at the person or item in your imagination and decide to forgive them and yourself for any unresolved hurts, anger or other negative emotions. Forgiveness is not an emotion, but a decision to release yourself from a negative attachment.
5. Release the person or item in your imagination, allowing them to go and do or be whatever they choose. They can choose to stay, and you can choose to allow them to stay, but without the negative attachment.
6. Thank and bless the person or item in your imagination.

5. Do The Work

The Work by Byron Katie is a process that can help you identify negative emotions and attachments and find freedom. There are several free downloadable worksheets at http://thework.com/dothework.php including the Judge Your Neighbor Worksheet, the One Belief at a Time

Worksheet, and the Emotions List. There are videos demonstrating the process and links to find a certified facilitator if you wish to work with someone who can help you release fear, ego and other negative emotions.

6. Create Accountability

Fear and ego can be very isolating. Find an accountability partner or a mentor who will hold you responsible for the changes you want to implement. Share your dreams and vision with this trusted individual and allow them to speak encouragement and positive proof into your life. Choose this person with care, making sure they are reinforcing the behaviors you wish to change.

CHAPTER 9

PURSUING PURPOSE

[pur-p*uhs*] The reason for which something exists or is made; an intended result or aim.

"Definiteness of purpose is the starting point of all achievement."
W. Clement Stone

You were designed for a purpose. You—with all your specific strengths, skills, and experiences—were designed to fulfill a specific purpose. Only you can fulfill that purpose. **The clearer you are on your purpose, the more likely it is that your life will have direction, focus, and satisfaction.**

Without purpose, life holds no meaning. There is no clear sense of direction or focus. Decisions are made randomly or are based on our moods. Without purpose, our passions run dry. Work is tedious, and life seems very hard. At the other end of the continuum, passion and purpose out of control becomes fanaticism. Fanaticism is an obsessive purpose that refuses to be contained with appropriate boundaries. This chapter will explore how to find clarity about your purpose, how to cure hopelessness and how to avoid unhealthy fanaticism.

Later in this chapter you'll see how Marcy's belief in her purpose helped her get through some hard times. Keeping her focus on her passion was the key. Clarity on his purpose helped a man move from despair to hope. He realized he could create the life he always wanted, and living that life has allowed him to reclaim his health and his family. **Purpose is the reason "why" we do what we do.** Passion, which is closely associated with purpose, fuels the energy we need to keep going when things get tough. **A strong sense of passion-driven purpose gives us the confidence to take leaps of faith and fulfill our destiny.**

What is Purpose?

Before you can find and fulfill your purpose, it is important to understand what purpose is. A lot of writing and research has been done on this topic, and it seems to me that most authors have captured just one or two facets of the complete jewel that is purpose. It is not that purpose is that complex, but that every aspect of purpose is valuable for thought and reflection.

After observing successful people like Albert Einstein and Eleanor Roosevelt, psychologist Abraham Maslow developed a theory of self-actualization, and defined it as "the full use and exploitation of talents, capacities, potentialities, etc."[1] What he was describing was the process of developing and utilizing all of our gifts, talents, strengths and experiences to **become the best version of ourselves that we can be**. Much of the human potential or personal growth movement revolves around Maslow's ideas. Maslow said, "I think of the self-actualizing man not as an ordinary man with something added, but rather as the ordinary man with nothing taken away."[2] The process of becoming a fully self-actualized man or woman means moving away from basic or self-centered desires (e.g., self-esteem, connectedness, security, and physical needs) and moving towards the ideals of morality, creativity, compassion and critical thinking. The process of self-actualization is not our purpose for existence. It is an important part of equipping ourselves to fulfill our purpose.

Rick Warren started his bestselling book *The Purpose Driven Life* with the statement: "It's not about you."[3] His point: People sometimes confuse purpose with self-actualization. We have a very human drive to fulfill our potential and we can spend hours on end on self-improvement. But to what end? Purpose is much more than pursuing our best selves. **Purpose transcends the self and leads us to what some have experienced to be an awakening or enlightenment.** Finding clarity on your purpose, destiny or calling can be a simple "aha" moment or a deeply mystical experience. This is because purpose is the intersection of your physical experience, your spiritual path, and your emotional core.

In his book *The Power of Now,* Eckhardt Tolle shifts the focus of purpose off the future and on to the present moment. In his zen-like manner, Tolle talks about how our purpose is found in being.[6] Your purpose in this moment is reading this page. Mine is writing this book. In another moment, my purpose is to stop to take a sip of water. When I stop and notice the shape of the glass in my hand, the coolness of the water on my tongue, and the sensation of my thirst being satisfied, I experience my purpose in that moment. Tolle's words remind me of the Psalmist's reminder to "Be still and know that I AM God."

Purpose is found in the silence of this present moment and your vision of the future. **Purpose is about the journey and not the destination.**

> *"Without a vision the people perish."*
>
> *Proverbs 29:18*

Why should you believe in and pursue your life's purpose? Purpose gives us hope. Hope is the confident expectation that things are going to be just fine. Without hope, there is no motivation to move forward. Purpose gives us direction as we move forward, and focus to stay on the path. Hope alone is not enough to keep us moving in the right direction. Once we begin to move forward, purpose generates and is fueled by passion. Purpose is guided by core values, and those values help us maintain the integrity of our path. These five traits: hope, direction, focus, passion and values are essential to success.

> *"The purpose of life is a life of purpose."*
>
> *Robert Byrne*

Life Without Purpose

Viktor Frankl was a psychologist who described the essence of life purpose in his book *Man's Search for Meaning.*[4] This book was based on Frankl's experiences in a Nazi concentration camp during World War II. The original book was written in German, and the title can be translated into English as *Yes to Life in Spite of Everything: A Psychologist Experiences the Concentration Camp.*[5] This attitude of saying "Yes to Life" describes the perspective of transcending the good and bad of this life to fulfill our destiny. According to Frankl, the meaning of life is found in every moment of living and that there is always someone (a family member, an authority figure, or even God) we do not want to disappoint with the way we choose to live that life. It was the memory of his wife that drove Frankl to hang on to hope. No matter how cruelly he was treated, Frankl knew he needed to live up to and for something greater than the present moment. Frankl's experiences in the Nazi death camps help us better understand how important purpose is in the midst of suffering. Life is not always easy—but life without purpose is unbearable.

> *"Man can live about forty days without food, about three days without water, about eight minutes without air, but only for one second without hope."*
>
> *Hal Lindsey*

The Importance of Hope

Hope is highly underrated when you consider creating success in life and business. Hope has been proven to be an important component in achieving goals. Dr. Shane Lopez is a positive psychology researcher with the Clifton Strengths School who defines hope as "the energy and ideas that drive people to change their circumstances." When asked by the Gallup Business Journal why hope was so important Dr. Lopez replied, "**Hope keeps us in the game**. With low hope, we stop interacting with the world. We pull back. Literally, we don't show up."[7] According to Dr. Lopez, hope forms when "goals thinking (I want to go from here to there) combines with pathways thinking (I know many ways to get from here to there), and agency thinking (I think I can get from here to there)."[8] The Hope Formula below might help make this process clearer:

HOPE =

Goals Thinking (What I want)

+

Pathways Thinking (What I know about getting there)

+

Agency Thinking (What I believe I can do)

Hope is deflated when any part of the formula is missing. Consider **Agency thinking**. When you believe you can create change you are experiencing agency thinking. Fear plays a destructive role in the Hope Formula. You can be afraid to want, afraid to try, afraid to fail. A lack of belief in your ability to create the change you desire and achieve your goals was discussed in Chapter 3. This lack of belief is often due to negative self-esteem. The antidote to this negative outlook is resilience. Resilience is essential to hope, for it is a resilient spirit that gets up again and again to pursue a goal regardless of what anyone else says or does. Rebuilding resilience will strengthen your ability to hope, and therefore strengthen your sense of purpose.

> *"Our deepest fear is not that we are inadequate. Our deepest fear is that we are powerful beyond measure. It is our light, not our darkness that most frightens us. We ask ourselves, Who am I to be brilliant, gorgeous, talented, fabulous? Actually, who are you not to be? You are a child of God. Your playing*

> *small does not serve the world. There is nothing enlightened about shrinking so that other people won't feel insecure around you. We are all meant to shine, as children do. We were born to make manifest the glory of God that is within us. It's not just in some of us; it's in everyone. And as we let our own light shine, we unconsciously give other people permission to do the same. As we are liberated from our own fear, our presence automatically liberates others."*
>
> *Marianne Williamson*

In addition to believing that you *can* achieve your goals, you must have some idea of *how* to achieve your goals. **Pathways thinking** is the ability to generate and consider optional solutions. A sense of hopelessness can be created by feelings of incompetence, cluelessness and impossibility. Generating potential solutions requires an understanding of the problem. You will have more clarity about your purpose when you gain the knowledge you need to pursue your goals. This is probably the easiest part of the Hope Formula to repair, but only if you are aware of your lack of knowledge and are willing to go after that knowledge. Sometimes we don't know what we don't know. That is when we need others to give us objective feedback and constructive criticism. A willingness to receive instruction and the openness to new ideas is essential to Pathways thinking.

Goals thinking is the most difficult part of the Hope Formula to develop. To have hope, you need to want something. It is possible that you have given up on allowing yourself to want anything to change in your circumstances. When this kind of ambivalence or defeat has taken root, it is a challenge to eradicate it. It is a form of apathy and the cure is clarity on your values, vision and passions. Later in this chapter you will find tools to identify your values, define your vision, and perceive your passions. Embracing them will keep you from settling for anything less than all you were designed to be and do.

> *"Once you choose hope, anything is possible."*
>
> *Christopher Reeve*

For several years I worked on a suicide prevention hotline. Sometimes people would call simply because they were feeling sad or lonely and they just wanted to talk to someone. All too often I would get a call from someone serious about ending their life. My job was to get that person talking. As long as they were talking, they were not acting on the impulse to end their lives. I would gently probe until I found what had led them to the conclusion that life was no longer worth living. Some of my callers talked about their failures and how they had disappointed someone important to them. Others were desperate for attention, angry at the world that had failed to give them the love they needed. Most of them had fallen into a dark depression that prevented them from seeing any possible purpose in their existence. Hopelessness had turned to despair.

One night, very late, I received a call from a man who called himself Bob. He'd been standing there for hours in the cold, terrified of jumping to his death, but even more terrified of living. He had seen the crisis hotline number on a bench and decided to call because he didn't know what else to do. Bob was in his early thirties and had a problem with drugs. His addiction had led to the loss of his job and the respect of friends and family. His wife had filed for divorce and he was probably going to lose custody of his children. He couldn't think of anyone he could call except a stranger at the crisis center. Bob was disgusted with himself and didn't believe his life was worth saving. He told me over and over that he had nothing to live for. I waited for him to run out of words and then I asked him,

"What if your life's purpose hasn't even started yet?"

Bob was quiet for a moment and then softly asked me what I meant.

"What if the reason you're here this very moment is to experience this desperation so your kids see that someone can fall down and get back up again? What if your life is supposed to be a story of survival and victory?"

Bob let out a huge sigh, and then asked me how he could ever become the man he wanted to be for his children. We talked for a while about Bob's options, places he could get help and ways he could turn his life around. Then Bob asked me a question:

"Why do you take these calls? Why would you spend your time talking to people like me?"

The answer came easily. "I believe I was designed for a purpose, and that is to help other people find their purpose."

Bob was quiet so long that I wondered if he was sinking back down into depression, but then he told me he wanted to live. We sent a police patrol car to pick him up and take him to the hospital. Bob entered a drug rehab program and began to rebuild his life. A few months later I was working at the crisis center again and got another call from Bob. This time it was to thank me for talking him off the bridge. He told me that the idea that his purpose was still out there waiting for him gave him hope. Bob had a new goal. He wanted to show his kids that he could overcome the challenges he was facing. Bob also told me that the counseling he had received in rehab helped him find clarity on the pathway to his goals. When Bob agreed to treatment, he was determined to become an agent of change in his own life and the lives of his children. Goals, pathways, and agency added up to hope. Hope was all he needed to start on the path to purpose.

> *The future belongs to those who believe in the beauty of their dreams.*
>
> *Eleanor Roosevelt.*

Jack Canfield tells a story about a little boy raised in poverty. His father was an itinerant horse trainer who moved his family from place to place, living out of a camper pulled by a beat up pickup truck. His education was constantly interrupted as he transferred from school to school. During his senior year, the boy was given an assignment to write a paper about what he wanted to be and do after he finished school. He got to work immediately on writing a seven-page paper that described his dream of one day owning his own ranch. He added a drawing of where the buildings, stables and track would be. And then he drew a detailed floor plan of his dream house. It was 4,000 square feet and sat in the middle of his 200-acre dream ranch. He put his heart into his project and then turned it in to his teacher.

When he got his paper back he was shocked to find a big red letter 'F' at the top with a note, 'See me after class.' The boy stayed after class and asked his teacher, 'Why did you give me an 'F'?'

The teacher explained, 'This is too unrealistic a dream for a boy like you. You have no money. You come from an iterant family. There is no way you could ever find the resources to buy the land, the breeding stock and the stud fees to have a ranch this size. If you rewrite your paper, I will consider changing your grade.'

The boy went home and thought about it long and hard. He asked his father what he should do. His father said, 'Look, son, you have to make up your own mind on this. However, I think it is a very important decision for you.'

The boy turned his options over in his mind for several days before turning in the same paper with no changes at all. He told his teacher, 'You can keep your 'F'—I'll keep my dream.'

This story is true. Monty Roberts is a friend of Jack Canfield's, and he has that paper with the big red 'F' framed, hanging above the fireplace in his 4,000-square-foot home in the middle of his 200-acre horse ranch in San Ysidro, California. Monty loves hosting groups at his ranch, and a few years ago he had his former teacher visit the ranch with a group of students. When the teacher was leaving, he said, 'Look Monty, I can tell you this now. When I was your teacher I was something of a dream stealer. During those years I stole a lot of kids' dreams. Fortunately you had enough gumption not to give up on yours.'[9]

Never let go of your dreams!

Passion and Purpose

Monty Roberts was and still is passionate about his horse ranch. That passion was a deep yearning, a nearly obsessive interest, a feeling or belief that without it his life would somehow be incomplete. What is your passion? What are the desires of your heart? How well does the life you're living now match up with your ideal dream life?

All too often we let go of the dreams we had as children and settle for "real life." Somewhere along the line we get practical, face our limitations, and do what is expected of us. Years later we find ourselves dissatisfied with life and wondering "what if?" A popular song asks thought provoking questions:

> *"Yesterday is a wrinkle on your forehead.*
> *Yesterday is a promise that you've broken.*
> *This is your life, are you who you want to be?*
> *This is your life, is it everything you dreamed that it would be?*
> *When the world was younger and you had everything to lose?"*[10]
>
> *Switchfoot*

Somewhere along the line you may have been given the impression that it is wrong to follow your passions or the desires of your heart. These passions can seem impractical and pursuing them may look self-centered. The truth is that it is wrong to ignore your passions. Your passions are Divinely inspired, given to you to guide you toward your unique purpose.

Chris Attwood and Janet Bray Attwood are on a mission to turn passion statistics upside down. A Gallup poll done in 2009 revealed that only 30 percent of workers are

- doing work they love doing work they love
- feel energized and enthusiastic about their work
- receive the recognition and support they desire.

This means 70 percent of workers are disengaged and dispassionate about their work.[11] This lack of passion in the work place eats away at an organization, spreading from one employee to another like a virus. Most people spend about half of their waking hours at work, and for most people this time is spent doing things they don't love. In their book *The Passion Test,* Janet Bray Attwood and Chris Attwood outline a process for discovering your top five passions and how to live life guided by those passions.[12] They have also created *The Passion Test for Business* and are helping transform organizations to create a culture where employees are fully engaged, pursuing their passions and seeing how those passions are in alignment with the mission and vision of the company.[13] It is a powerful process, and it changed my life forever.

> *"Let yourself be silently drawn by the stronger pull of what you really love."*
>
> *Rumi*

Unlike most workers, I was fully engaged in my private coaching practice when I first went through *The Passion Test* process. I was pursuing what I believed was the purpose of my life: "helping executives and entrepreneurs find and fulfill life's purpose." I loved my work, but it consumed all of my focus, energy, and time. My life was out of balance. I had put everything else on hold in order to build my business. I also struggled with knowing how to prioritize aspects of my work. Should I spend most of my time coaching individuals or groups, or should I do more speaking? Or should I spend more time getting my book done? I felt torn and unclear about how to use my time. Knowing your passions and pursuing them not only gives you clarity on your purpose in life, but it also helps you live a full, balanced life with priorities that fit your personal and spiritual values.

The Passion Test for Business has been designed to help solo-entrepreneurs and large corporations create a vision and strategy for their companies guided by passion. Because of the huge impact *The Passion Test* had on my life, I was ready for the new insight and clarity this tool might offer.

I was asked to write down ten things that completed the sentence, "When my work is ideal, I am ______________." I wrote down things like facilitating personal and spiritual growth, speaking to large audiences, publishing a best-selling book, a steady stream of grateful clients who placed a high value on our work, traveling the world, and enjoying financial freedom to the point where I could support the people and causes I believe in. As I wrote, I realized I was unclear on how to define who and what I was. Am I a coach? A speaker? A writer? I wasn't sure. That's when I had an incredibly important insight:

Living a passionate, purpose-filled life isn't about doing and having everything you want; it's about being everything you want.

The concept of the importance of BEING rather than DOING or HAVING was not new to me. The life transforming idea was this: that my passions would lead me closer toward being the person I was designed to be, regardless of the label. Those deep desires of the heart are like beams of light leading us to greater understanding of who we are and what we are here to do.

Like a lot of people, I struggle with over thinking things when what I need to do is listen to my heart. I believe I fall back on logic and rational thought to protect me from making emotional choices, but this is not helpful when trying to get in touch with your passions. I believe many of us have been taught to ignore our noisy inner child jumping up and down with excitement and delight. Instead we strive for a more mature, restrained approach. Discovering your passions and purpose requires that you stop rationalizing away what you want. It means:

Living a passionate, purpose-filled life means listening to your heart and not your head.

This concept of being led by your heart rather than your head may be hard for some of you to hear. I know I was raised to view my emotions with skepticism and to use my mind to make decisions. Listening to your heart does not mean casting reason aside and blowing back and forth on the winds of emotion. Making wise choices about your life requires that you consider the deepest longings of your heart. This is not something that can be analyzed. Your mind will quickly find at least six ways something can't be done as soon as your heart suggests something new or challenging. Quieting your thoughts and letting your heart speak will allow hope to grow and vision to emerge.

When I completed *The Passion Test for Business* I was surprised to see that writing this book was a higher priority for me than any other activity in my business, including coaching. Right away I felt fear grip my heart. If I focused on writing, how would I keep cash flowing since coaching was my primarily source of income? If I spent most of my time writing, how would I get to the networking meetings and speaking events that generated new clients? I had wanted to write this book for several years, but I kept putting it off. I realized I was missing out on something special. My next insight was:

Living a passionate, purpose-filled life eludes us when we let fear and hopelessness control our lives.

Once I accepted that writing this book was to be the central focus of my work that year, I began to get excited. I began to see how the book would generate new programs and materials for coaching. I recognized how I would have more material for presentations. I saw that I would be able to market myself more effectively as I had greater clarity and focus for my work. For every question my rational mind threw out, my heart found a creative solution.

I set an intention that I would write a book that had a broad reach and strong impact on people's lives. I had originally planned to self-publish but then something remarkable happened. I won a publishing contract with Hay House/Balboa Publishers through the Transformational Authors Contest. Winning this contest has given my book broader reach and support than I ever could have imagined. It helped me understand an insight that I've heard Janet Attwood say over and over again:

"When you are clear, what you want will show up in your life, and only to the extent that you are clear."[14]

Entering a writing contest was the furthest thing from my mind, but then I remembered the secret to a passionate life:

"Every time you are faced with a choice, decision or opportunity, choose in favor of your passions."

When I chose to focus on my book and enter the Transformational Authors Contest, I set things in motion that have changed the focus and success of my work forever. Even before its publication, material from *Your Belief Quotient* has been used in coaching sessions, presentations, and has sparked creative ideas for future products and services. Having clarity in your work and business is essential to success. Choosing in favor of your passions in your work and your life will lead to greater freedom and creativity. Your heart will lead you to solutions you never would have thought of.

There is a reason why I've shared these stories about me finding and marrying my husband (in Chapter 8) and the background for getting this book to print in such detail. Before I discovered my top five passions for my life and my business, I thought I was fulfilling my purpose. I was spending hours every day serving people and building a business where I could serve more. I loved my work. But the rest of my life was empty. I had set time with friends and family aside. I had stopped writing and performing music. I had no time for artistic or creative projects. I wasn't active physically and didn't get outside much. I didn't have time or money for travel. I was attending church regularly, but did not feel connected. I was confused about my business strategy. I struggled with defining my niche. I didn't have a clearly defined marketing plan. My life was transformed when I put one simple sentence into practice:

"Every time you are faced with a choice, decision or opportunity, choose in favor of your passions."

Every day I seek to choose in favor of my passions and in the order of how my passions are ranked. Having a system for decision making will give you greater confidence in your choices and keep you on the path to fulfilling your purpose.

Choose your regrets. In addition to making choices based on passion, asking yourself which choice would you regret more is a powerful way to move from your head to your heart. If an opportunity appears to travel to a place you've always wanted to see, ask yourself which you would regret more, never seeing that amazing place or the expense of the trip. If you know you would regret the cost of the trip more than the experience, then skip the trip. But if you are sure that you would always regret missing the trip even if it meant sacrificing to go, you need to listen to your heart. Ask yourself if in 5, 10 or 25 years which decision would you be glad you made? You will regret something. It is best to choose your regrets.

Passions shift and change over time. Regardless of whether you use the Passion Test or another process, I highly recommend assessing your passions every six months. Clarity on your passions allows you to live and work with assurance and conviction about your purpose. Knowing the order of your passions will help you to prioritize strategically and to recognize and take advantage of opportunities without distraction. This is how passion fuels purpose.

In his book, *True Purpose*, Tim Kelley offers guidance on discovering your purpose. He talks about soul influences that guide us toward purpose.

- Intuition: In moments of quiet reflection, or moments of crisis, some people can sense a part of themselves that is calm and unperturbed by events. They can sometimes "hear" advice or wisdom at these times.
- Synchronicity: Chance coincidences are sometimes too "convenient" or meaningful to be true accidents. Your soul can arrange meetings or events to give you a message.
- Crisis: When you ignore your purpose and the direction your soul wants you to go, it can arrange difficult situations for you. These can range from minor inconveniences to true crises.
- Learning Experiences: In service to your "training", your soul can create circumstances that will force you to develop and learn. The ego usually dislikes these challenges, as they are disruptive to its goals.[14]

Your heart will be heard. The easiest way is to listen to your intuition or "your gut". There is a sense of knowing that can be trusted. You come to a fork in the road and just sense that you should turn left. Learning to trust your intuition is a skill worth developing. Your heart also will use your brain as a filter, finding the connections and coincidences in life that seem somehow guided or planned. Driving along the road you keep seeing the same car, even after stopping along the way. Upon arriving, you discover the driver was headed to the same event you were. If you fail to notice the synchronous events or follow your intuition, your unconscious mind can create conflicts to get your attention. It is as if your mind is dropping a guard rail in front of you to prevent you from driving in front of a train. Ignore the guard rail, and an even greater challenge can be generated by your mind. When things in your life come crashing down, know that there are occasions where suffering is a tool designed to guide us back on the right road toward the fulfillment of our purpose.

Purpose Gone Wrong—Fanaticism

"Convictions are more dangerous foes of truth than lies."
Friedrich Nietzsche

When our beliefs about our purpose become skewed we fall into fanaticism. Fanaticism has been defined as "excessive, irrational zeal; wildly excessive or irrational devotion, dedication, or enthusiasm; an extreme and uncritical zeal or enthusiasm, as in religion or politics; excessive intolerance of opposing views."[9] Key words in this definition are "excessive" and "irrational". **Your purpose should be fueled with a burning passion, but when that passion is consuming, you risk becoming unbalanced**. Fanatics have trouble respecting boundaries and often offend others. In their zeal for their beliefs, they may even think they should offend in order to make a point and stand firm. Fanatics have no need for popularity, for they are convinced they are right and that is all that matters.

You can be a fanatic about religion, politics, fitness, fiscal responsibility, or almost any ideal. Passion for any of these things is good, and pursuing your purpose in these areas is the right thing to do if that is your calling. Be conscious of how your passion for your ideals is affecting others. Seek to persuade, convince and influence—but never badger, mock or repudiate someone simply because they don't agree with your views.

I grew up in a very conservative church. I used to joke that we made Jerry Falwell look liberal. Looking back, I now see that this church was filled with good people who had fallen into the trap of not thinking for themselves. They had become legalistic, judgmental, and narrow minded. The young people in our church were taught to believe that no other denomination had it quite right. If you befriended people from other churches you were putting yourself at risk of being led astray. We were told what kind of Bible to carry, how long to wear our skirts and hair, what music to listen to, and what books to read. Women were not allowed to speak or teach, men were the leaders in the assembly, and God hated divorce. Somehow I learned at an early age to separate my relationship with God from my relationship with the church. This kept me from rejecting religion and spirituality completely. Eventually I realized that all this power and control came from fear. The leaders of our church were afraid to let us think and decide, to explore and make mistakes. Fundamentalism used to mean believing in the fundamental doctrines of faith, but in many groups it has become fanaticism. Religious fanaticism is easily identified in extremist groups, but its destructive effect can be seen in any faith community.

I am thankful for the spiritual foundation that was laid in my life. I still treasure the scriptures and spiritual principles that guide me in life's choices. After I became disillusioned with the church I was raised in, I made a spiritual journey studying the teachings of other denominations and several religions. This was a scary time for my family who was sure I was at risk of being deceived. Instead of weakening my faith, this journey served to strengthen my connection to God and my personal commitment to my spiritual growth. Now I find myself active in a church that I know is not conservative enough for some people, and way too conservative for others. What I love about my faith and the church where I worship is that there is freedom. People are accepted regardless of their mistakes or controversial opinions.

I am equally thankful that I learned to recognize the destructive force of fanaticism. It isn't enough for a fanatic to hold strong opinions, but they are compelled to convert everyone around them. Fanatics are not just found among the religious. There is nothing more obnoxious than someone who has found health and fitness and has become more than an evangelist for healthy eating and supplements. The Food Nazi judges the choices of others and condemns them loudly. Every four years the United States faces contentious political ads and rhetoric, where fanatics from one party or the other harp on their viewpoints whether anyone is listening or not. The fanatic is so caught up in their drive to convince that they do not see how their arrogant, unkind, controlling, manipulative behavior destroys their relationships and credibility.

There is a fine line between passion and fanaticism. That boundary line is objectivity. Recognizing that you are not responsible for the choices of others is essential. Accepting that everyone has the right to learn at their own pace is important. **Embracing the possibility that there is the slightest chance that you could be wrong is crucial.**

Balanced Values

One of the hallmarks of fanaticism is a failure to live with balanced values. The religious zealot is so busy focusing on judgment and condemnation of sinful behavior that he has forgotten grace, peace and love. The Food Nazi has become so rigid that she has forgotten the benefits of flexibility. The political fanatic is so confident in his solutions to the country's problems that he has lost the values of tolerance, empathy, and openness to learning new ideas.

For every value, there is balancing value. Keeping balance in your values and beliefs will help prevent you from falling into fanaticism. Here are a few examples of balanced values:

Excellence .... Productivity
Discipline ....Flexibility
Frugality .... Generosity
Justice .... Mercy

As you see, every one of the values above is a positive quality. However, focusing too much on one end of the spectrum can lead to a lack of balance, and possibly to fanaticism.

Pursuing Purpose

> *"The purpose of life is to discover your gift.*
> *The meaning of life is to give your gift away."*
>
> *David Viscott*

Finding and fulfilling your life purpose is a process of self-discovery. Before you can serve the world with your gifts, you need to know what those gifts are and how you uniquely express them. Dr. Donna Markova writes:

> "When we find ourselves devoid of passion and purpose, the first thing we need to do is stop. But that's not easy. The rest of the world is zooming by at full speed. Left alone with ourselves, without a project to occupy us, we can become nervous and self-critical about what we should be doing and feeling. This can be so uncomfortable that we look for any distraction rather than allowing ourselves the space to be as we are . . . To explore what it would mean to live fully, sensually alive and passionately on purpose, I have to drop my preconceived ideas of who and what I am."[15]

You have been told who you are all your life. Some of what you've been told is accurate, but some of it has been cruelly limiting. Shaking off false beliefs of who you are and the gifts you possess will empower you to pursue your purpose with joy.

There are a wide variety of tools available for this journey of self-discovery. I have already mentioned the Myers-Briggs Type Indicator[16], Strengthsfinder[17], spiritual gifts inventories, and The Passion Test.[18] These are tools that I use with clients and have benefitted from personally. This chapter started with the declaration that you were designed for purpose. With that design comes all the resources you need to fulfill that purpose. But you must choose to take action to use those resources and do the work you were called to do.

> *"We yearn for our independence not just so we can go where we want to and speak up when we want to, though that feels good. But that's child's play and ego-driven. The deeper part of us yearns to create, to fulfill whatever it is we were born to do—and that requires we take charge of our own power of choice. Meaning and purpose is driven by the engine of choice, make no mistake about that."*
>
> *Caroline Myss*

Life Purpose Statement

> *"Writing or reviewing a mission statement changes you because it forces you to think through your priorities deeply, carefully, and to align your behaviour with your beliefs."*
>
> *Stephen Covey*

As you choose to fulfill your purpose, making choices based on passion and using the gifts and talents you were given as resources, you will want a clear sense of why you do what you do. A Life Purpose Statement can provide that clarity. A Life Purpose Statement, or what Stephen Covey calls a personal mission statement, can be a beacon of light that guides you and keeps you from drifting from purpose. The statement defines success—how will you know you have fulfilled your purpose? It states what you believe is important, outlining key values and principles that guide your life. It is a unique statement that is all your own, because no one else has exactly the same purpose as you.

There are three key questions to consider in crafting your Life Purpose Statement:

- **What** do I want to **do**?
- **Who** do I want to help?
- What is the **result**? What value will I create?

Marcy is an excellent example of someone who lives by their personal mission. After completing *The Passion Test* and working through the *Belief Quotient* in coaching, Marcy was not surprised that her top passion and priority are her children. She is one of those mothers who truly enjoys her children. Whenever she gets the chance, she plays with them, makes music with them and connects with them on a heart level. Marcy started her business so she could leave a demanding job with late hours to be home with her kids. That business fulfills other passions she has for creativity and organization, but the reason it exists is to support her children and give her the freedom to raise them to be healthy, productive adults. Narrowing down all she does to this statement of purpose gives her reason to keep going when times get tough. Marcy's purpose statement gives her a sense of pride and accomplishment as she sees progress in her children's lives.

What will be your life's contribution? How are you changing the world? What is your purpose?

> *"Never let your dreams die in the daylight. Arise each day and sculpt the day purposefully like an artist, making it your own. Fight for what you believe in. Honor the struggle as something that is good and necessary and important in summoning and stretching the very best in you. Victory is close. Victory is close. Victory is close."*
>
> *Brendan Burchard*

EXERCISES for Pursuing Purpose

1. Who You Really Are—Complete the following sentences in your journal:

- If I could do anything I wanted, I would . . .
- If I could be who I wanted to be, I would . . .
- If I could play any part, it would be . . .
- If I could help people, I would . . .
- If I knew myself, I would . . .
- When I discover what I want to do, I will . . .
- The purpose of my life is . . .
- I am here on Earth to . . .

2. Create a Strategic Plan—For Life & Work

Create a road map for how you want to get from here to wherever your vision is taking you. Start with the big picture and then determine what steps you need to take to get there. Each action step should be clearly defined and the expected outcome should be something you can measure. There are great tools for creating a strategic plan, including the ***GPS for Life and Business*** you can find on my website at www.lisavanallen.com.

3. Prioritize

Do what's important first. The distractions of email, text messages, and reality TV shows can keep us from focusing on what is truly important. In order to spend time on activities that support your life's vision and keep your daily life in better balance, consider these productivity tips:

- Have a scheduled time for emails and social media so they do not dominate your day.
- Get up fifteen minutes earlier to set the day's intention and meditate on your vision.

- Write a list of the things you need to and want to accomplish for the day. Limit this list to 3-5 key activities.
- Work in spurts by scheduling Power Hours where you work on a single task without distraction for a full hour. Stop for a break, and then, if you wish go for another hour. Do not attempt to do more than 2-3 Power Hours in one day as your ability to focus will diminish.
- Be on the outlook for time-wasters, such as web surfing or lingering on social media sites, instead of addressing the items on your to-do list.
- Know what you value most in life and then spend more time there.

4. Reflect

Take ten minutes at the end of each day to reflect on your day's activities. Examine the things that made you feel successful and happy compared to those that contributed to anxiety and stress. Look for patterns from one day to the next. Living a balanced life is about identifying and doing more of what is working and less of what is not. Consider whether your actions and thoughts support your vision and passions.

- List three things that are going well. Write down the qualities that contributed to this success.
- List three things that are NOT working in your life. Write down what you need to change accordingly. Use the POWER acronym described in previous chapters to decide on a course of action if it is helpful to you.

5. Journal using the reflection questions below:

1. What are you for?

   It's easier to say what we're against. But what about what you stand for?

2. For whom do you live?

   To know your purpose is to be impassioned by doing work that in some way, big or small, makes things better for others, not simply for yourself.

3. What personal values guide you?

   Knowing your personal values will guide you through the good and challenging times in your life and business.

4. What engages your imagination?

   Reflect back on work you've done. What captured your imagination? What freed you up to try something new? Purpose can be found in unlikely places or obvious ones.

5. What are you willing to do without?

   Living a life of purpose and passion makes the lean times better.

6. What do you expect from yourself?

   Attempt to answer this question without perfectionism or low self-esteem.

7. What if you weren't afraid?

   Are you emotionally ready to take on living life on purpose?

8. What's possible?

   What's possible if you can get out of your own way?

9. How scared are you?

   How white are your knuckles? Where are you feeling out of control?

10. What question would you add?

6. Look Ahead and Look Back

Imagine that you are celebrating your 90th birthday. You are sitting on a rocking chair outside on your porch enjoying the day. Looking back at your life and all that you've achieved and acquired, all the relationships you've developed; what matters to you most? List them out.

7. Create Measures

Allow yourself to reflect on your progress toward purpose and define measures that will indicate that progress. How will you know you are living out your purpose? Create a set of metrics that are both markers along the way as well as goals for behavior.

Example: If part of your purpose is to serve others, the metric could be the number of hours you volunteer or the amount of money you raised.

8. Draft your Life Purpose Statement

Begin crafting your Purpose Statement, but keep in mind that this statement will continue to grow and change as you do. You might find Franklin Covey's Mission Statement Builder helpful: http://www.franklincovey.com/msb/

CHAPTER 10

STRENGTHENING NEW BELIEFS

"If you don't change your beliefs, your life will be like this forever. Is that good news?"
Dr. Robert Anthony

Imagine you are a pioneer traveling in a new land. No map exists for this strange place, but you are given a blank piece of paper to draw your own map as you travel down streets and roads . . . Your perceptions are skewed because you do not have the whole picture . . . You did the best you could, but you know the picture you have is lacking. Your map is flawed with false assumptions and misperceptions.

This is where we started in chapter 1, with the beginnings of belief: a blank piece of paper on which you create your life map based on experiences and perceptions. But what if you could climb a hill to get a better view of the countryside? What if you had a better sense of direction and knowledge of some of the pitfalls along the way? Your journey would be much easier. You would arrive at your destination with fewer bumps and bruises and detours.

It is my hope that this book offers you a bird's eye view for your journey toward better beliefs. From your perch on the mountain you can see these key points:

Beliefs are the lens through which everything you experience is filtered. Your personal belief system plays a decisive role in how you view and create success. Resistance to changing beliefs is to be expected as your brain tries to protect you from change.

You can't fix something that you are unaware is broken. The Belief Quotient Assessment was designed to help you identify weakened or skewed beliefs. Once those beliefs have been identified, you can work through the chapters and exercises to build better beliefs.

Use the POWER acronym to create behavioral change that will change your beliefs:

P — What is the **problem** I am facing? Am I clear about what I want to shift?

O — What are my **options**? Is surrender necessary, or can I continue on as I am? How are these beliefs showing up in my day-to-day life?

W — How will I **work** on and practice my new skills? What specifically am I going to do to create change?

E — How will I know I am improving? How will I **evaluate** my progress?

R — What will I do to **reinforce** my progress and **reward** my success?

Put **POWER** to work for you as you change your Belief Quotient. Complete the exercises at the end of each chapter. Look for opportunities to get objective feedback on your progress and create accountability for your growth.

You tend to inherit certain patterns of brain behavior from your family. These patterns can be overcome by identifying faulty beliefs and intentionally building better beliefs. The brain is changed chemically by beliefs, thoughts, feelings and behaviors produced by the mind. You can change your brain!

Holding the belief that you are resilient and *not* a victim to your past or present circumstances is the foundation to your success. Taking personal control and responsibility for your reactions and behavior is necessary to rebuild resilience.

Connectedness is that ability to create and sustain meaningful, mutually beneficial relationships with others and yourself. You need to develop and maintain healthy boundaries with others, with yourself, and with your God to enjoy connectedness. Once you have rebuilt resilience and established healthy boundaries you are ready to open your heart to receive and respond with compassion, vulnerability, and authenticity.

Initiative is the ability to begin or to follow through energetically with a plan or task; it includes enterprise and determination. Initiative is the result of passion, purposeful planning, and clarity on your ideal life and work.

Excellence is a process of becoming and depends upon a belief that you can keep reaching and growing to achieve your objective. Perfectionism is not excellence when it means picking at something over and over. When you set high personal standards and maintain them, you create a stronger sense of well-being and confidence.

Abundance is the belief that there is more than enough. Having faith in an abundant universe that conspires for your good is a belief held by the most successful people in the world. Individuals who have an abundance mindset are ready to receive the blessings and joys coming their way. There are 7 Universal Laws of Abundance that, when applied, create the flow of abundance in our lives under any circumstances. The infinite supply of abundance is channeled through the character of God Himself and communicated to us by grace. Regardless of your spiritual beliefs, this gracious gift of abundance is available to you. Just as the rain falls on all of us, abundance is accessible to everyone.

Faith is a belief that drives behavior due to the complete surrender to mental acceptance of an idea. Faith is an internal belief that does not rely on external evidence for confirmation. When we "run toward the lions" and refuse to shrink in fear, we test and prove faith works.

Purpose is the reason "why" we do what we do. The clearer you are on your purpose, the more likely it is that your life will have direction, focus, and satisfaction. Hope is an essential aspect of purpose. The Hope Formula is Goals Thinking (What I want)+ Pathways Thinking (What I know about getting there) + Agency Thinking (What I believe I can do)

Your passions are Divinely inspired, given to you to guide you toward your unique purpose. The secret to a passionate life is "Every time you are faced with a choice, decision or opportunity, choose in favor of your passions." Studies show measurable results, better outcomes, more passion and greater joy in every area of life when people find and seek to fulfill their purpose.

Next Steps

So where do you go now on your journey to better beliefs? First I suggest you find a supportive community of people who are committed to creating healthy belief systems. At www.beliefquotient.com we will be hosting discussions and opportunities to interact with others on this path. Join us!

Second, you might consider hiring a coach or mentor who can hold you accountable for completing the exercises in this book and applying the principles in practical ways in your life.

Finally, watch for additional resources from Van Allen & Associates and the authors quoted in this book. Make building better beliefs a lifelong quest!

I want to leave you with a final word of encouragement that has impacted my own life. It is my prayer for you.

Long before God laid down earth's foundations,
He had us in mind,
had settled on US as the FOCUS of His LOVE,
to be made whole and holy by His love . . .

It's in Christ that we find out **who we are**
and what we are living for.

Long before we first heard of Christ and got our hopes up,
He had His eye on us, had designs on us for
GLORIOUS LIVING,
part of the overall purpose
He is working out in everything and everyone.

I ask the god of our Master, Jesus Christ, the God of glory
to make you **intelligent** and **discerning**
in knowing Him personally,
your eyes FOCUSED and CLEAR,
so that you can see
exactly what it is He is calling you to do,
grasp the immensity of this GLORIOUS way of life
He has for His followers,

Oh the utter **EXTRAVAGANCE** of His work in us
who trust Him—
endless energy, boundless strength!

Ephesians 1: 4, 11-12, 17-19, The Message

RESOURCES

Definitions at the beginning of each chapter were taken from www.thefreedictionary.com, Farlex Inc., 2012.

Unless otherwise noted, Bible references all come from the New International Version, Zondervan, 1993.

Chapter 1

1. Lund, F. H., "The Psychology of Belief," The Journal of Abnormal and Social Psychology, Vol 20(1), Apr 1925, 63-81; 174-195.
2. Asch, S. E. "Effects of group pressure upon the modification and distortion of judgment." In H. Guetzkow (ed.) *Groups, leadership and men*. Carnegie Press, 1951.
3. Amen, Daniel; Wu, Joseph C.; Bracha, H. Stefan. "Functional neuroimaging in clinical practice." *The Comprehensive Textbook of Psychiatry* edited by Kaplan and Sadock 2000.
4. Amen, Daniel, *Change Your Brain, Change Your Life*, Three Rivers Press, 1999.
5. Seligman, M. E. P., *Helplessness: On Depression, Development, and Death*, W. H. Freeman, 1975.
6. Seligman, Martin, "Australian Psychologist." *Coaching and Positive Psychology*, 2007.
7. Fredrickson, B. L., Mancuso, R. A., Branigan, C., & Tugade, M. M., "The undoing effect of positive emotions." *Motivation and Emotion*, 2000.
8. Frederickson, Barbara L., *Positivity: Top-Notch Research Reveals the 3-to-1 Ration That Will Change Your Life*, Three Rivers Press, 2009.

9. David Kiersey and Marilyn Bates, *Please Understand Me: Character and Temperament Types,* B & D Books; 5th edition, 1984.
10. Adler, Alfred, *Understanding Human Nature:* The Psychology of Personality, Ed. Colin Brett, Oneworld, Reprint edition, 2009.
11. Dispenza, Joe, *Evolve Your Brain: The Science of Changing Your Mind,* HCI; Reprint edition, 2008.
12. Seligman, Martin, *Flourish: A Visionary New Understanding of Happiness and Well-being,* Free Press, 2012.
13. Attwood, Janet Bray and Chris Attwood, *The Passion Test*, Plume, 2008.

Chapter 3

1. Anderson, Mac, *The Power of Attitude*, Thomas Nelson, 2004.
2. Marquez, John, *The Ultimate Journey*, CL Ministries, 2009.
3. Norris, F., Tracy, M., & Galea, S., *Looking for resilience: Understanding the longitudinal trajectories of responses to stress.* Social Science & Medicine 68 2190-2198, (2009).
4. Seligman, M. E. P., *Development, Helplessness: On Depression and Death,* W. H. Freeman, 1975.
5. Frankl, Victor, *Man's Search for Meaning*, Pocket Books, 1988.
6. Grohol, J. (2010). 15 Common Defense Mechanisms. *Psych Central.* Retrieved on April 10, 2012, from http://psychcentral.com/lib/2007/15-common-defense-mechanisms/
7. Tedeshi, R. G., and L. G. Calhoun, *Trauma and Transformation: Growing in the Aftermath of Suffering*, Sage, 1995.
8. Beck, Martha, "Yes, It Was Awful—Now Please Shut Up," *O Magazine,* July 2006.
9. Kosfeld, Michael, et al, "Oxytocin Increases Trust in Humans", *Nature,* Nature Publishing Group, 2005
10. McGonigal, Jane, "The Game that Can Give You 10 Extra Years of Life," http://www.ted.com/talks/lang/en/jane mcgonigal_the_game_that_can_give_you_ 10_extra_years_of_ life.html.

11. Van Allen, Lisa, "Build Better Beliefs with Affirmations," http://lisavanallen.wordpress.com, May 2, 2012.
12. Canfield, Jack, *The Success Principles*, William Morrow, 2006.
13. Mitchell, Stephen and Katie, Byron, *Loving What Is: Four Questions That Can Change Your Life*, Three Rivers Press, 2003
14. Oswald, Yvonne, *Every Word Has Power*, Atria, 2008.

Chapter 4

1. Brown, Brené, "Vulnerability", http://www.ted.com/talks/brene_brown_on_vulnerability.html, 6.22.12.
2. Brown, Brené, "Listening to Shame", http://www.ted.com/talks/brene_brown_listening_to_shame.html 6.22.12.
3. Umberson, Debra, and Jennifer Karas Montez, "Social Relationships and Health," *Journal of Health and Social Behavior*, Nov 2010.
4. *The Diagnostic and Statistical Manual of Mental Disorders*, Fourth Edition Text Revision, American Psychiatric Association, 2000.
5. The ICD-10 Classification of Mental and Behavioural Disorders, World Health Organization, Geneva, 1992.
6. Beattie, Melody, *Beyond Codependency*, Hazelden Foundation, 1989.
7. Levinger, G., "Development and Change" H.H. Kelley, et al. (Eds.), *Close relationships*, W.H. Freeman and Company, 1983.
8. Cloud, Henry and John Townsend, *Boundaries*, Zondervan; Revised edition 1992.
9. Canfield, Jack, *Success Principles*, Harper Collins, 2005.
10. Buckingham, Marcus, *Go Put Your Strengths to Work*, Free Press, 2007.
11. Silver, Mark, "Some Serious Sufi Woo-Woo in Sales," http://www.heartofbusiness.com/2010/sales-woo-woo/ 6.27.12
12. Ruiz, Don Miguel, *The Four Agreements*, Amber-Allen Publishing,1997.

Chapter 5

1. Erikson, Erik, *Childhood and Society*, Norton 1963
2. Rath, Tom, *Strengthsfinder 2.0*, Gallup Press; 1 edition, February 1, 2007.
3. Kiersey, David and Marilyn Bates, *Please Understand Me:Character and Temperament Types*, B & D Books; 5th edition. 1984.
4. Hogan Personality Inventory, http://www.hoganassessments.com/hogan-personality-inventory, 6.30.12.
5. Reiss, Steven, *Who Am I? The 16 Basic Desires That Motivate Our Action and Define Our Personalities*, Tarcher/Putnam, 2000.
6. Ryan, Richard and Edward Deci, "SelfDetermination Theory and the Facilitation of Intrinsic Motivation, Social Development and Well-Being," http://www.psych.rochester. edu/SDT, 6.18.12.

Chapter 6

1. Institute of Medicine, *Sleep Disorders and Sleep Deprivation: An Unmet Public Health Problem,* The National Academies Press, 2006.
2. Amen, Daniel, *Making a Good Brain Great,* Harmony Books, October 2005.
3. Nideffer, Robert M., "Getting Into the Optimal Performance State," http://www.taisdata.com/articles/optimal.pdf, 6.20.12.
4. Nideffer, Robert M., "Getting Into the Optimal Performance State," http://www.taisdata.com/articles/optimal.pdf, 6.20.12.
5. Tatarkiewicz, Wladylaw,_"Perfection: the Term and the Concept," *Dialectics and Humanism*, vol. VI, no. 4, Warsaw University Press, Autumn 1979.
6. Leonard, Thomas, The Portable Coach, "Perfect Your Environment", Scribner, 1998.

Chapter 7

1. Covey, Stephen, *The Seven Habits of Highly Effective People*, Free Press, 2004.
2. Chapman, P. J. and Gertrude A. Catlin, "Growth Stages in Fruit Trees-From Dormant to Fruit Set," *New York's Food and Life Sciences Bulletin*, No. 58, February 1976, Cornell University.
3. *NIV Study Bible*, Zondervan, 2011.
4. Covey, Stephen, *The Seven Habits of Highly Effective People*, Free Press, 2004.
5. "U.S. Trust 2012 Insights on Wealth and Worth Survey of High Net Worth and Ultra High Net Worth Americans 2012 Highlights," Bank of America Corporation, 2012.
6. Twenge, Jean, *Generation Me: Why Today's Young Americans are More Confident, Assertive, Entitled and More Miserable Than Ever*, Free Press, 2007.
7. *NIV Study Bible*, Zondervan, 2011.
8. *The Amplified Bible*, Zondervan, 1983.
9. Tracy, Brian, *The 100 Absolutely Unbreakable Laws of Business Success*, Berrett-Kohler Publishers, 2000.
10. Ponder, Catherine, *The Dynamic Laws of Prosperity*, Prentice-Hall, 1984.
11. Rosenthal, R., and Lenore Jacobson, *Pygmalion in the Classroom*, Holt, Rinehart & Winston, 1968.
12. Attwood, Janet Bray and Chris Attwood, *The Passion Test: the Effortless Path to Discovering Your Life's Purpose*, Plume, 2008.
13. Tracy, Brian, *The 100 Absolutely Unbreakable Laws of Business Success*, Berrett-Kohler Publishers, 2000.
14. Matthew 13:3-23.
15. Oswald, Yvonne, *Every Word Has Power*, Atria Books, 2008.
16. Cialdini, Robert B., Noah J. Goldstein and Steve J. Martin, *Yes! 50 Scientifically Proven Ways to be Persuasive,* Free Press, 2008.
17. Canfield, Jack, *The Success Principles*, William Morrow, 2006.

Chapter 8

1. David Kiersey and Marilyn Bates, *Please Understand Me: Character and Temperament Types,* B & D Books; 5th edition, 1984.
2. Armstrong, Karen, "Faith and Modernity," Retrieved on November 16, 2012 from http://www.worldwisdom.com/ public/viewpdf/default.aspx?article-title=Faith_and_Modernity_by_Karen_Armstrong.pdf.
3 Macquarrie, John, *Thinking About God,* London, 1957.
4 Hill, Napoleon, *Think and Grow Rich,* Sterling, 2012.
5. Hebrews 11:1, New King James Version, Thomas Nelson, 1982.
6. LaPorte, Danielle, *The Firestarter Sessions,* Crown Publishing, 2012.
7. Hill, Napoleon, *Think and Grow Rich,* Sterling, 2012.
8 Dispenza, Joe, *The Habit of Being Yourself: How to Lose Your Mind and Create a New One,* Hay House, 2012.
9. Romans 10:17, *New King James Version*, Thomas Nelson, 1982.
10. Hill, Napoleon, *Think and Grow Rich,* Sterling, 2012.

Chapter 9

1. Maslow, Abraham, *Motivation and Personality*, Harper-Collins, 1987.
2. Maslow, Abraham, and Richard Lowry, *Dominance, Self Esteem, Self Actualization*, Thomson Brooks, 1984.
3. Warren, Rick, *The Purpose Driven Life*, Zondervan, 2002.
4. Fankl, Victor E., *Man's Search for Meaning: An Introduction to Logotherapy*, Beacon Press, 2006.
5. Frankl, Victor E., *Trotzdem Ja Zum Leben Sagen: Ein Psychologe Erlebt das Konzentrationslager (Saying Yes to Life in Spite of Everything: A Psychologist Experiences the Concentration Camp)*, Kosel, 1979.

6. Tolle, Eckhardt, *The Power of Now,* New World Library, 2004.
7. "Why Hope Matters Now," *Gallup Business Journal,* Gallup, Inc., 2012.
8. Lopez, Shane, and C.R. Snyder, *Oxford Handbook of Positivbe Psychology*, Oxford University Press, 2009.
9. Canfield, Jack, and Mark Victor Hansen, *Chicken Soup for the Soul: 101 Stories To Open The Heart And Rekindle The Spirit,* HCI, 1993.
10. Switchfoot, "This is Your Life," *The Beautiful Letdown,* Sony/BMG, 2003.
11. "Employee Engagement: What's Your Engagement Ratio?" Gallup Consulting, 2008.
12. Attwood, Janet Bray, and Chris Attwood, *The Passion Test,* Plume/ The Penguin Group, 2007.
13. Attwood, Chris, Janet Bray Attwood, and Beth Lefevre, *The Passion Test for Business Consultant Certification Manual,* Enlightened Alliances, 2011.
14. Kelley, Tim, *On Purpose,* Transcendent Solutions Press, 2009.
15. Markova, Dawna, *I Will Not Die an Unlived Life*, Conari Press, 2000.
16. David Kiersey and Marilyn Bates, *Please Understand Me: Character and Temperament Types,* B & D Books; 5th edition, 1984.
17. Rath, Tom, *Strengthsfinder 2.0,* Gallup Press; 1 edition, February 1, 2007.
18. Attwood, Janet Bray, and Chris Attwood, *The Passion Test,* Plume/ The Penguin Group, 2007.

INDEX

A

Adler, Alfred | 12-14, 17, 230
Amen, Daniel | 6, 131, 229
Angelou, Maya | 51
Anger | xiii, 5, 51, 56, 63, 64, 100, 133, 150, 187, 188
Anthony | Robert, 223
Anxiety | 56, 63, 80, 83, 157, 193, 219
Apathy | 14, 44, 111, 202
Aristotle | 129
Assaraf, John | 21
Attwood, Janet Bray and Chris | 18, 160, 206, 209, 230

B

Beck, Martha | 64, 230
Boundaries | xv, 10, 62, 78, 84, 86-89, 99, 105, 194, 197, 212, 225, 231
Breathnach, Sarah Ban | 145
Brown, Brené | 78, 81, 231
Buckingham, Marcus | 98, 231
Burchard, Brendan | 217
Byrne, Robert | 200

C

Canfield, Jack | 74, 204, 231

Carnegie, Dale | 112
Choprah, Deepak | 61, 166
Chekhov, Anton | 1
Churchill, Winston | 167
Cialdini, Robert | 165, 233
Cloud, Henry | 86, 231
Codependence | 81
Coolidge, Calvin | 167
Covey, Stephen | 145, 148, 150, 216, 233

D

Defense mechanisms | 58-60, 62, 66, 79, 230
Dependence | 78-79
Dispenza, Joe | 15, 180, 189, 230

E

Edelman | Marian Wright, 119
Einstein, Albert | 102, 170, 198
Entitlement | 14, 101, 147, 150-151, 194

F

Fanaticism | 197-198, 212-215
Fear | xv, 2, 15, 21, 44, 55, 60, 63, 68, 70, 79, 80-81, 86, 95, 101, 110-111, 112, 113, 116, 121, 134, 138, 147, 156, 163-164, 168, 178, 180-183, 185, 186-187, 189, 192, 195, 201, 208, 213
Flowers, Betty Sue | 99
Frankl, Victor | 200, 230, 234
Frederickson, Barbara | 8, 65, 229

G

Gibran, Kahlil | 91

Goethe | 121

H

Hill, Napoleon | xiii, 74, 179, 189, 234
Hopelessness | 5, 58, 198, 203, 209

I

Isolation | 14, 78-80

J

Jakes, T.D. | 188

K

Katie, Byron | 72, 194, 231
Kelley, Tim | 211, 235
Kiersey, David | 230, 232, 235
King, Jr., Martin Luther | 77
Kloser, Christine | 183, 185
Kubler-Ross, Elizabeth | 84

L

Lamott, Anne | 136
Laporte, Danielle | 181, 191
Law, Michael | 138
Lawhead, Stephen | 188
Lefevre, Beth | 182
Levinger, George | 82-83, 231
Lindsey, Hal | 200
Lopez, Shane | 200-201, 235

M

Markova, Donna | 215
Marquez, John | 55-56, 230
Maslow, Abraham | 198, 234
McGonigal, Jane | 66, 230
Myss, Caroline | 216

N

Nideffer, Robert | 133, 232
Nietzsche, Frederich | 212

O

Osteen, Joel | 186

P

Passion Test | 18, 159-160, 182, 206-208, 211, 215, 230
Pearsall, Paul | 61
Perfectionism | 11, 96, 111, 114, 129, 135-140, 225,
Ponder, Catherine | 154, 168
POWER (acronym) | 18, 20, 43, 121-122, 127, 170, 224

R

Reeve, Christopher | 202
Remen, Rachel | 78, 164
Robbins, Anthony | 109, 169
Roberts, Monty | 205
Rodgers, Buck | 130
Rohn, Jim | 116, 123
Roosevelt, Eleanor | 198, 204
Rumi | 207

S

Seligman, Martin | 8, 17, 229
Scarcity (mindset) | xv, 14, 147-150, 155, 158, 164
Solis, Brian | 94
Stone, W. Clement | 197
Strengths (StrengthsFinder 2.0) | 23, 25, 36, 38, 88, 95-96, 112, 133, 151, 175, 197, 200, 215, 231, 232
Swindoll, Charles | 55
Switchfoot | 206

T

Temperament (Myers-Briggs Temperament Indicator) | 8-9, 84, 96, 178, 230, 232
Tolle, Eckhardt | 199
Tracy, Brian | 153, 162, 170, 233

U

Unconscious mind | xiv, xv, xvi, 1, 4-5, 7, 17-19, 20-22, 57-60, 67, 96, 148, 163, 189, 202

V

Victim/victimization | xv, 10, 14, 54, 56, 57, 58, 61-63, 66, 70, 89, 224
Viscott, David | 215

W

Warren, Rick | 199, 234
Williamson, Marianne | 201-202

CPSIA information can be obtained at www.ICGtesting.com
Printed in the USA
LVOW120037210213

320996LV00001B/67/P